268/350

ISBN: 978-1-7346325-0-7 (Hardcover)

Front cover image by Amy T. Won
Book design by Amy T. Won

Printed in the United States of America.

An Explorer's Journal of Wonder-Walking

A Guidebook for Reconnecting to Nature & Your Creativity

Written & Illustrated by Amy T. Won

Table ⁹ᶠ Contents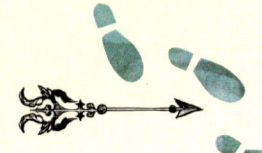

Prologue

*There are truths and stories awaiting me on paths outside
my door. I've only to step out and listen hard.*

A Story of Wonder-Walking

My Dearest Wonder-Walkers,

Once upon a time, a few years ago, I was weary and depleted in
spirit. I was at the crossroads of my creative practice, having
left an old path behind and uncertain of my artistic future. I
was burnt out from pouring my heart and soul into a creative
business I no longer wanted to advance and disconnected
from my own voice as an artist. I felt like everyday life was
bleached and colorless. I had lost my creative sparkle and
studio time was painful.

Slowly, I began creating a world to heal and nourish my
creative soul. And I started walking. A little every day, with my
camera and a miniature rabbit toy.

Short walks. Long walks. Walks in the neighborhood. Walks
in the hills. And my spirit began to heal. Soon I was painting
again. Some days I ran back to the studio to put brush to
paper. I slowed down and began noticing details around me I
had never noticed before.

I began to develop a way of seeing the world all my own.
Ideas and color came back into my life like watercolor paint
blooming on wet white paper.

I realized now what I didn't know back then: wonder-walking
is tremendously healing. It slowed me down and helped me
see the magic in my everyday. It reconnected me to my inner
and outer worlds and made me feel more alive than I'd felt in
a long time. And so I kept at it.

Over the years I've learned to find my own rhythm of wonder-walking - favorite places and times of the day, what to bring along and when, how and when to photograph, paint or write what I notice.

Some days everything I encounter on a walk feels straight out of Fairyland, and other times, it's drab and brown as far as the eye can see. Some of my best walks have been really short strolls out with my camera, or when I've conquered lethargy to step out the door. Often the most healing walks have taken place after a busy, stressful time away from the outdoors.

There have been walks that stole my breath and left me speechless in awe, and other walks that had me counting each step till our destination.

While it isn't necessary to own *A Deck For Wonder-Walking* to enjoy meandering outdoors, I've found it useful for resetting my tired lens and battling one of my biggest obstacles to adventuring - inertia. I don't always feel like going outside for a walk, a run, or a bike ride, and so it's precisely these times that I reach for the cards. After all, incentive is why I created the deck in the first place.

And every time I pull a card for a walk, I feel centered, I see the world anew in fresh, exciting ways. I am re-inspired. And so I wrote the guidebook I needed myself. A place to explore the vast potential of the cards and to remember all the different ways wonder-walks light up my everyday - the big and small acts of joy and discovery, the unexpected stumbles upon delight, the difficult but invaluable experiments in discomfort. A lifetime of being a child and a child-at-heart spilled into these pages.

In the end, what emerged is a deeply personal, contemplative guidebook written from my own adventures that I hope you'll dip into for life, over and over again in a never-ending cycle of re-enchantment.

Much love,
Amy T. Won

PART I
A Magical World

The Wonder-Walk

*Learning to see with fresh eyes and a beginner's mind,
to fall in love over and over with the ordinary, day after day,
is vital for the creative soul.*

T he world is magical. It really is. But somewhere in the dark corners of my mind, I have this deep-seated fear of wandering life with my gaze downward, finally looking up one day, some years in the distant future, disoriented and heartsick to find I'd missed out on its many marvels when I wasn't paying attention.

And so I wonder-walk, believing whole-heartedly that this simple practice can halt a gradual disconnection from my physical environment and reverse the easy acceptance of digitally mediated interactions. What's more, I've discovered with relief through my walks that wonder, curiosity, imagination and mystery, rather than becoming relics of a lost time, can be joyfully restored.

The Wonder-Walk is any intentional exploring that reconnects us with our tangible world, re-invigorates our senses and creativity, and makes us come alive.

It's an invitation to not only look closer and immerse deeper into the places we inhabit, but also to know ourselves in it. It requires no tools to begin, beyond our own two feet and a child-like determination to notice and delight in the little things, to see the world anew everyday.

But a wonder-walk is more than just a walk in nature or a mindful experience. It is a participation. A belonging. An awakening. It is cultivating a relationship between our inner and outer worlds, where boundaries dissolve and magic flows freely.

A wonder-walk can be a simple 20-minute daily practice in the neighborhood with your dog, or a 5-minute moving meditation in a serene park. It's everything from the 2-hour scenic hike along the coastal bluffs to the 3-minute walk from the grocery store to your car. Our state of mind (and heart) is more important than where or how our wonder-walks happen. Adventures are often nourishing day-long wonder-walks incorporating picnics, tours, strolls or shopping trips.

Wonder-walks are extremely inclusive activities. It doesn't matter if we live in isolation in a beautiful countryside, a tiny apartment in a crowded city, or in a suburban house with a yard; as long as we have our own two feet, we can venture out with our senses on alert, ready to embrace the treasures of the fascinating outdoors. Everything from the honeysuckle vines right outside our door to the cat-shaped mailbox down the street, to the sun filtering through the tree foliage has the potential to bewitch and amaze us in unexpected ways.

The list of artists and creatives throughout history who walk is long, star-studded, and varied, a quick look at the book Daily Rituals: How Artists Work by Mason Currey will provide ample inspiration! Both Thich Nhat Hanh, a spiritual leader, and Julia Cameron, renowned creativity teacher, extol the benefits of walking on the human spirit.

In this book, I often talk about walking as the physical bipedal activity we know and love so well, but ultimately for me, wonder-walking is an allegory for enchanted living, a healing return to our origins. It encompasses all the experiences, actions, and loving we do as humans in our craving for connection, meaning and rapture.

I hope that the wonder-walking and adventure ideas in this guidebook take you to marvelous places beyond your imagination, inspire many creative endeavors, and most importantly, restore a sense of magic and aliveness to your everyday.

How to Begin Wonder-Walking

An Explorer State of Mind

Be open, inquisitive and child-like. Explore as if everything is brand new and requires full attention, untainted by expectation and judgment.

Pull a Walking Card

The wonder-walks in this guidebook expand on the prompts of the corresponding card deck - archetypal words that emerged from my own journey of creative rejuvenation. Follow its magical breadcrumb trail to discover your own path to re-enchantment.

The Beautiful Inquiry:

Question everything. Challenge what you know. Wonder as you wander. Adopt beginner's mind. Ask why, what, when, how. Indulge your curiosity.

How to Use This Explorer's Journal

This guidebook is meant to tickle your imagination and nudge your sleeping explorer's spirit. It's by no means an exhaustive list of wonder-stoking, but rather, a jumping-off point for discovering your own quirky path to amazement. Here are suggestions on how to begin.

Option A: The Labyrinth Sequence

1. Start with the Physical Realm cards. The objective of the Physical Realm is primarily to step outside and engage the senses. It's the low-hanging fruit of wonder-walks but no less impactful. The easiest of the 4 Realm cards to wander with, the prompts, observations and activities in this section focus mainly on inspiring mindful presence on your walks.

2. Next, move on to Creative Realm cards. As you get comfortable with walking in nature, noticing and being present, incorporate creative tools to capture your experiences outdoors; a sketchbook, a field journal or notebook, a camera. Inspired by your walks, document how things appear (representational), or abstract them according to your feelings and ideas using the activities in this section as a springboard.

3. Once you've practiced mindful walking and have begun recording and expressing what you experience, we move on to the Inner Realm cards. If you're like me, by now you would be itching to make sense of what your walks are telling you about yourself, your place in the physical world, and how it mirrors your journey in life. This section dwells on self-reflection, meaning-making and accessing your unconscious as it relates to your walks. Use the cards, prompts and activities to dive below the proverbial waters and form a deeper connection with nature and the world around you.

4. Last but not least, we arrive at the final section, the Influence Realm. If you've been having fun experiencing, documenting and contemplating your walks, you should now have a vibrant picture of how you relate to the world around you. It's the perfect time to study what others have written, created and documented to further enrich your experiences. Use this section to explore how museums, books, art, history, etc. can inspire more wondrous walks.

Option B: Dipping

Use the book like you would an activity book from childhood, or your favorite cookbook. Depending on how you feel that day, pull a card from the deck (or a Realm) and dip into the book for the corresponding pages any time, non-chronologically. Some ideas to try:

⊙ Flip through the pages of the book until a page catches your eye with its colors, textures or symbolism. Pull the corresponding card, read the pages, and head out for your walk. Come back and journal on your own time.
⊙ Pick a Realm color that attracts you for the day. (green for Physical Realm, pink for Creative Realm, etc). Open the book to the corresponding Realm and select a card to walk with and work on that day.
⊙ Open the book with your eyes closed, and dip in randomly.

How to Use the Pages

Use the blank boxes throughout the Explorer's Journal to jot down big-picture ideas and thoughts that you want to remember for future adventures. Key places, wonder triggers or activities you discovered for yourself are good examples of what to record. Use a separate notebook for in-depth, exploratory journaling.

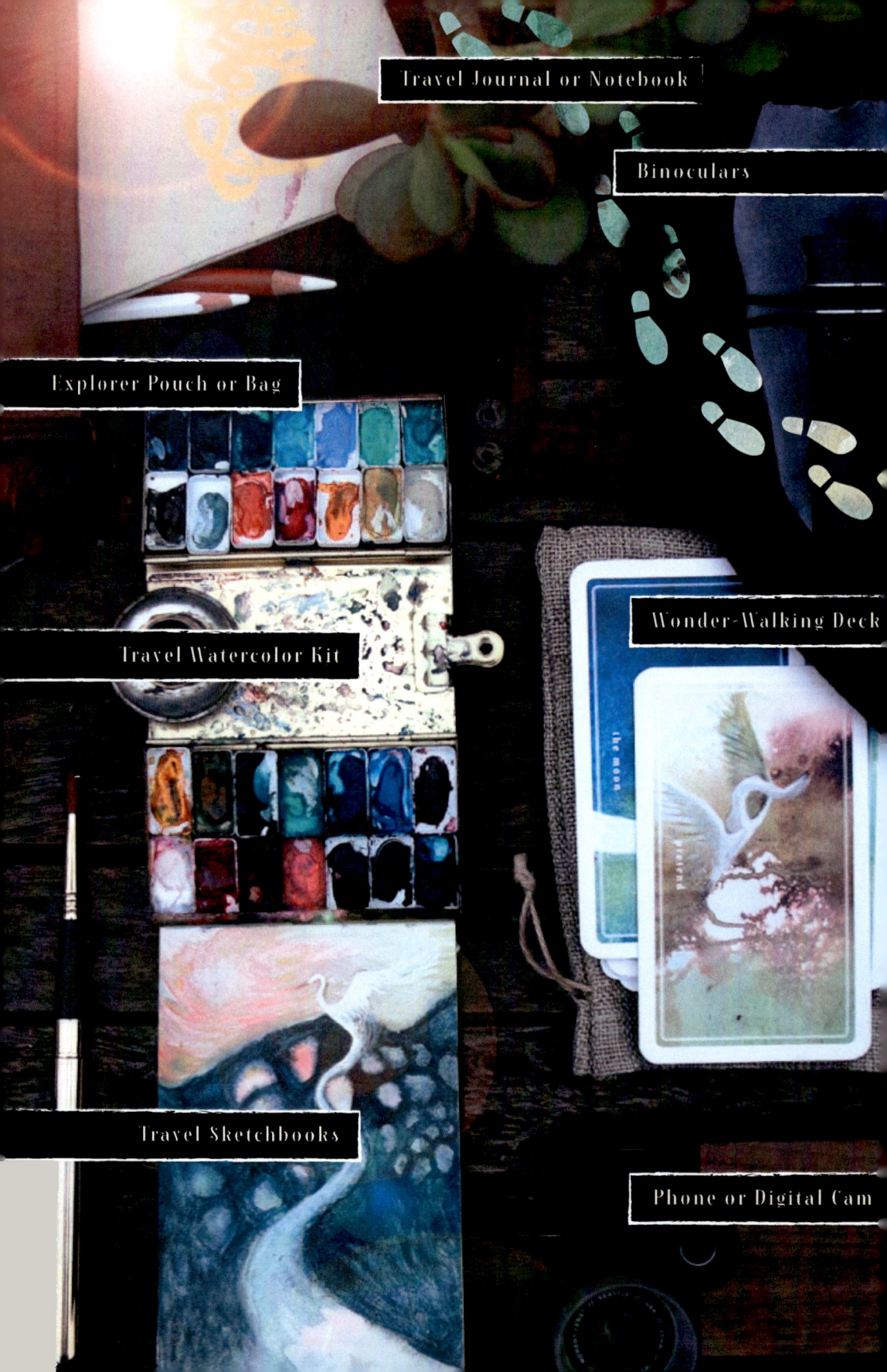

Travel Journal or Notebook

Binoculars

Explorer Pouch or Bag

Wonder-Walking Deck

Travel Watercolor Kit

Travel Sketchbooks

Phone or Digital Cam

What to Bring on a Wonder-Walk

Inspiration happens when we least expect it.

One of the beautiful things about wonder-walking is that we don't need anything more than our own two feet to immerse completely and soulfully into the land.

Nevertheless, there have been many times in the past when I've been caught empty-handed while on a walk and felt woefully unprepared. Fleeting moments when the dusk sky explodes into paintbox hues over the salt marsh, or a full moon rising like a large gold coin from behind the hills have left me arrested in enchantment, wishing I had my camera, my sketchbook, anything to capture the ephemeral glory before me.

Being Prepared For Inspiration

I've since learned to carry with me at all times, at least a small pouch containing my card deck and a travel watercolor kit, so that sudden moments of inspiration can be recorded and immortalized.

Eventually I began assembling what I call my Creative Adventure Kit, in various sizes, for different wonder-walking needs, so that I'm always prepared for nature's transient wonders. These kits can be anything from a simple, zippered explorer's pouch carried by itself or tossed into a larger everyday bag, or as complex as a waterproof knapsack with multiple pockets and hidden sections to keep all my explorer needs organized and protected from the weather.

My kits have also saved me from inertia many a time, when energy levels are low and everything from wonder-walking to painting feels like too much effort. Having my pouches and bags conveniently assembled and ready for adventure is one less obstacle out the door.

What Goes in Your Creative Adventure Kit?

In this section I'll lay out a few things you might want in your own Creative Adventure Kit, keeping in mind that it should be tailored to your wonder-walking needs.

As an artist, my needs are primarily creative in nature. I like to have my paints, pencil and sketchbooks at the ready so I can document any ideas and concepts that inevitably bubble up as my mind relaxes into the land when I walk.

Perhaps your walks serve a more healing purpose - a special time to be alone with your thoughts and dreams, and a little bit of respite from a challenging daily routine. You might find that in your case, a journal and a quality fountain pen is more important than a travel paint set.

When assembling a Creative Adventure Kit for your wonder-walks, ask yourself:

What are you hoping to get out of your wonder-walk?
Where are you going and how long will you be out? A few minutes, an hour, half a day, an entire weekend?
Will you be getting there by foot, by car, by bus or by bicycle?

Bags & Pouches
What would you use to carry your Creative Adventure Kit on your wonder-walks?

- Zippered pouches
- Cross-body sling bags
- Knapsacks or backpacks
- Hip pouches or fanny packs

Documenting & Recording
What would you need to capture your experiences, feelings and thoughts as you wander?

- Notebook and pen or pencil
- Sketchbook (small, medium or large)
- Digital SLR or polaroid camera

- ☉ Nature guide for trails, plants and wildlife.
- ☉ Phone with optional lens attachment
- ☉ A camera tripod is great if you're planning to take pictures of yourself, during sunset or of the starry sky at night.

Observation Aids

What instruments and tools can you bring along to alter or enhance your observations on your walk?

- ☉ Binoculars or monocular
- ☉ Telescope
- ☉ Magnifying glass or loupe
- ☉ Crystal prisms or balls
- ☉ Pinhole camera or toy camera
- ☉ Mirror

Creative Tools

What would you need to creatively express your experiences out in the field?

- ☉ Notebooks for writing or sketching - thinner papers
- ☉ Multi-media sketchbooks of different sizes and papers - heavier papers
- ☉ Zippered pouches with pencils, pens, watercolor palettes, painting cups
- ☉ Pochade boxes for 'plein air' painting.

Comfort & Nourishment

What can you bring along to make your longer walks or adventures more comfortable?

- ☉ Bento (lunch) boxes for snacks and meals
- ☉ Picnic blanket, jacket or wrap
- ☉ Thermos of tea or coffee
- ☉ Water bottle
- ☉ Hat to protect from the sun or cold
- ☉ Folding umbrella for rainy days
- ☉ Sunglasses to filter out glare and harsh light

What's in My Adventure Kit?

The Little Adventure Kit

Lives in the purse or everyday carry. Absolute essentials for wonder-walking anywhere. Minimalist.

Explorer pouch, Wonder-Walking Cards, brass magnifying glass (loupe), mini watercolor kit, waterbrush, small notebook, toy rabbit.

The Goldilocks Adventure Kit

Lives in a sling bag of its own, hangs by the door and easy to grab. The perfect little kit, not too big, not too small, just right for any length wonder-walk.

Little Adventure Kit above + travel sketchbook and notebook, pencils, DSLR camera and phone with lens attachment.

The Wanderer's Creative Adventure Kit

Best in a daypack. Be prepared is the motto here! This is the kit for longer walks and adventures - camping, stakeouts, road trips, and all manner of crazy, inspired-artist moments out of doors.

Goldilocks Adventure Kit above + large pouch with expanded water media and sketching tools, large sketchbook, extra notebook, extra camera lens, tripod, headphones, bento box, water bottle, a local nature field guide.

What's In Yours?

Essentials:

What's in your Little Adventure Kit?

Nice to Have:

What's in your Goldilocks Adventure Kit?

Serious Explorers:

What's in your Wanderer's Creative Adventure Kit?

The Physical Realm
WONDER & CURIOSITY

pareidolia
fairy worlds
flora
height
story
disruption
synesthesia
discomfort
roots
landmark
belonging
notice

The Creative Realm
MAGIC-MAKING

first love
textures
symbolism
mood painting
thumbelina
fauna
naiveté
play
dream
color
shape
dusk

The Influence Realm
SECRET GARDEN

the sun
poetry
journey
study
pretend
connect
follow the rabbit
immersion
memory
hidden
dawn
discernment

The Inner Realm
TRUTH-FINDING

spirit of place
enchantment
the woods
intuition
portals
the moon
home
wonder
listen
edges
darkness
fog

The Four Realms of Enchantment

What does it take to live a truly enchanting life?

It was a question my weary spirit posed to the universe one day, years ago, when I was at a crossroads, searching for something *more* in my creative practice. Though, like most soul truths, I must have already known the answer, because when I began exploring, I found myself intimately familiar with the path to enchantment.

Even so, I'd often wished I had a Field Guide to show me how to reliably return to this magical state whenever I needed to. It's so easy to slip into vicarious living through digital media and never tangibly experiencing for ourselves the splendor of wildflower fields or the simple joy of plein air painting. I pictured this Field Guide guiding me on an enthralling journey through a magical labyrinth in my psyche, passing through the four Realms of Enchantment: Wonder & Curiosity, Magic-Making, Truth-finding and the Secret Garden, hidden wonders unfurling like so many blossoming peonies along the way.

I imagined that somewhere along this interweaving soul journey through the Four Realms I would fall in love over and over again with all life has to offer.

The Labyrinth, The Symbolic Quartet & The Fourfold Correspondence

When I first envisioned the Labyrinth of Enchantment as the construct of my wonder-seeking mythology, I wasn't aware of its deep-rooted archetypal and symbolic correspondence with other fourfold worlds. Throughout the years of living and creating within it, I began to realize I had stumbled upon a rather

Text continues on Page 28

The Physical Realm •••••••••••• **WONDER & CURIOSITY**

Sensation
Earth
Material
Yin (Receptive)

Labyrinth of Enchantment

  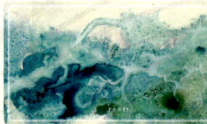

Thinking
Air
Intellect
Yang (Active)

The Influence Realm •••••••••••• **SECRET GARDEN**

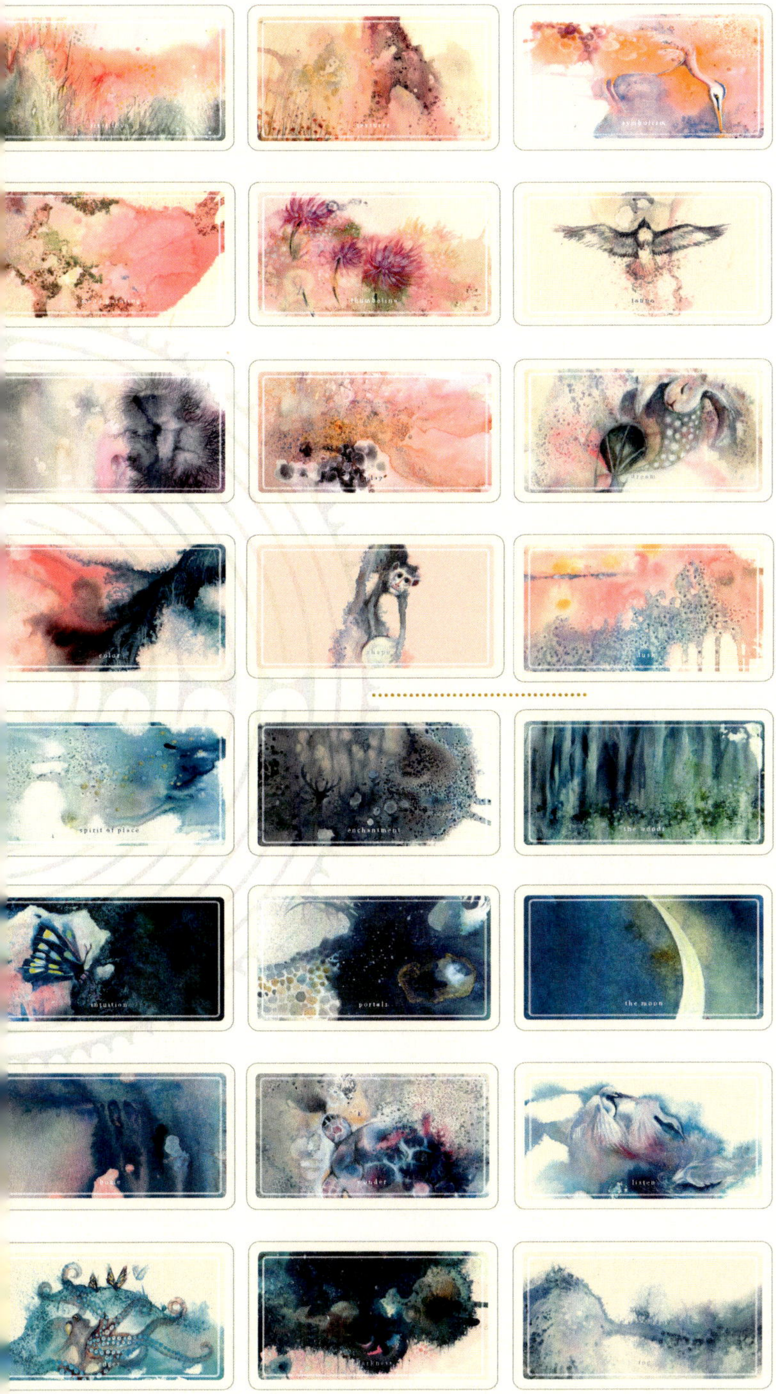

Symbolic Correspondence

MAGIC-MAKING ··············· **The Creative Realm**

Intuition
Fire
Passion
Yang (Active)

Feeling
Water
Unconscious
Yin (Receptive)

TRUTH-FINDING ··············· **The Inner Realm**

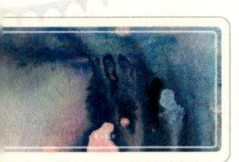

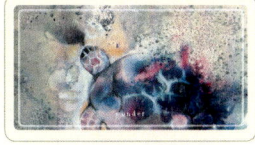

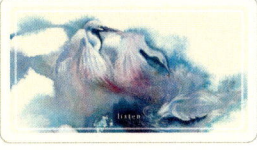

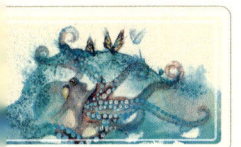

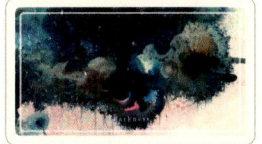

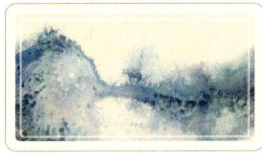

ancient and magical collective wisdom. I felt called to align what was in me with the existing quartets out there, suspecting that it would enrich and further enchant my own explorer's lens.

The Labyrinth's Realms slotted easily into Jung's four functions of Sensing (External Reality), Intuition (Subjective Reality), Feeling (Emotion) and Thinking (Reasoning). Likewise, they fit well with the alchemical elemental quartet of Earth, Fire, Water and Air.

The symbolism of Tarot's Minor Arcana came next. The only minor blip in this fourfold jigsaw puzzle came down to semantics. In Jung's original four functions, Intuition is the perceiving opposite of Sensation. Sensation for me corresponds to Wonder & Curiosity (Physical Realm), for it is the Realm where we allow our senses to roam free and play. Intuition, on the other hand, according to Jung, is a process that is both visioning, creative and interactive, which fits perfectly with Magic-Making (Creative Realm).

However, in most Tarot Minor Arcana symbolism, Intuition is related to the Suit of Cups (corresponding to the Truth-Finding - Inner Realm) In fact, Intuition is a walking card from this very suit in the deck! *In service of fourfold congruence and to avoid confusion, I'll have to preface by saying that the Intuition of the Creative Realm is related to the interactive creative process, while the Intuition card of the Inner Realm is related to that gut feeling, the unconscious bubbling, the elusive feeling of something coming up from our inner world.* All is inextricably interwined in reality of course, but within our symbolic construct, there are subtle differences.

A Labyrinth of Wonder-Walks

The previous pages show a diagram of your wonder-walking cards and various symbolic correspondences within their respective Labyrinth Realms. You might also notice that each Realm has an energy that is either Yin (receptive, feminine) or Yang (active, masculine). Fellow colorists like myself might note the subtle shift in color from one Realm to another, from cool earthly greens to passionate pinks, to emotional blues and illuminative yellows.

I like to think of the Realms (or suits) the cards belong to as adding a unique flavor or spice to the wonder-walk, beyond the word prompt on the card itself. Here's how each Realm flavors the cards within it:

Wonder & Curiosity: The Physical Realm

The Physical Realm is the domain of the senses and the exterior, material world. It corresponds with the Earth element. Cards in this Realm invite exploration through sensation, a Yin (receptive) experience. We take in information with our senses, allowing it wash over us like rain on a hot summer day.

Magic-Making: The Creative Realm

The Creative Realm is the domain of intuition, passion and subjective reality. It corresponds with the Fire element. Cards in this Realm invite an active Yang participation - of playfully capturing your wonder-walking experiences through photography, writing, painting or sketching.

Truth-Finding: The Inner Realm

The Inner Realm is the domain of feeling, emotion and the unconscious world within. It corresponds with the Water element. Cards in this Realm invite introspection and reflection, of allowing the exterior world encountered on wonder-walks to mirror your inner world, and with it, the truths you seek in the moment, very much a Yin (receptive) experience.

Secret Garden: The Influence Realm

The Influence Realm is the domain of thinking, reasoning and the intellect. It corresponds with the Air element. Cards in this Realm invite an active Yang study of your world. These

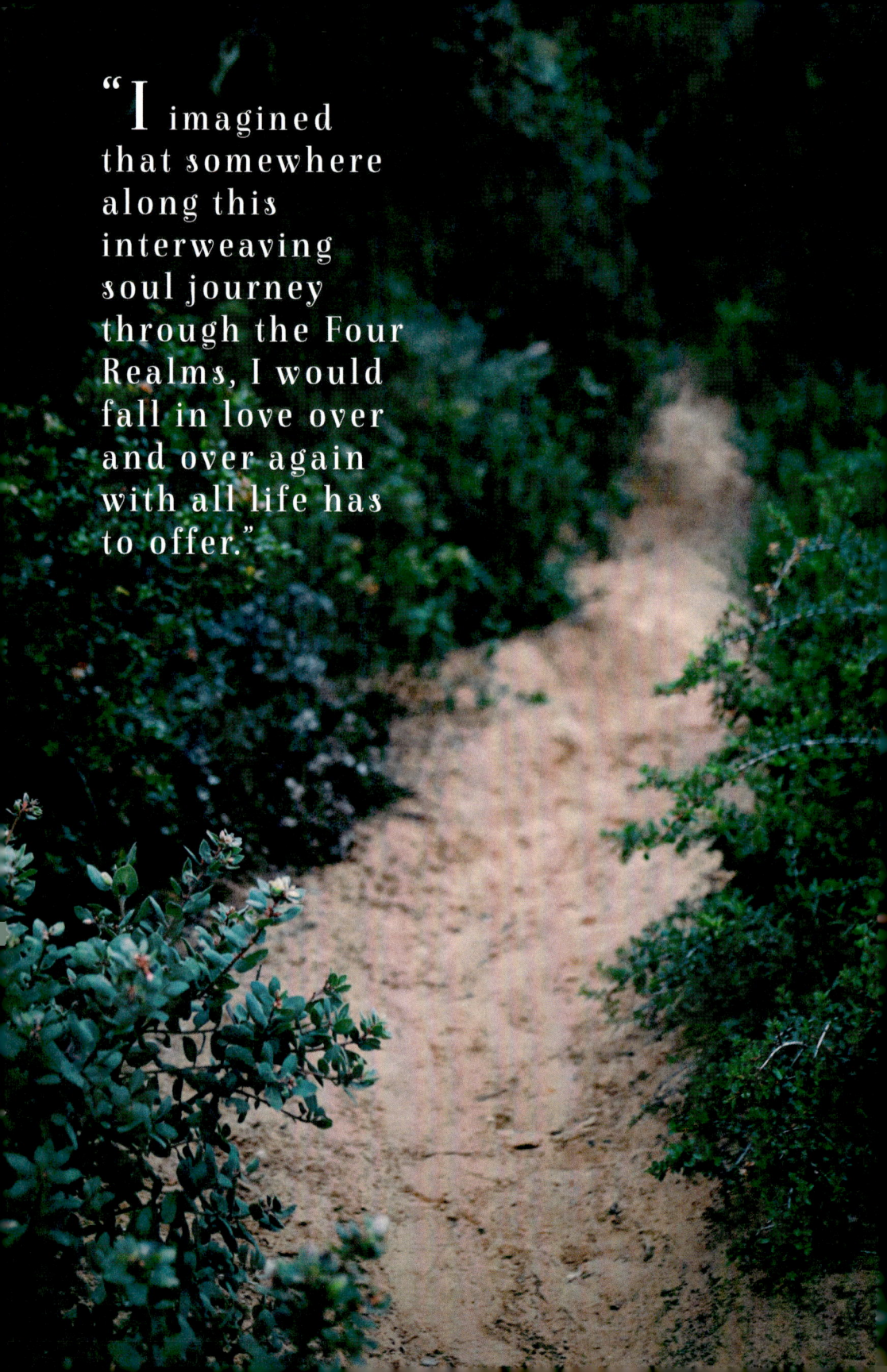

"I imagined that somewhere along this interweaving soul journey through the Four Realms, I would fall in love over and over again with all life has to offer."

wonder-walks are meant to immerse you in specific subjects and environments that inform, influence and illuminate your own understanding of the world.

Working With the Labyrinth Realms

In Chapter 1: The Wonder-Walk, I walked you through the Labyrinth Sequence method of using this guidebook with the corresponding cards - beginning with Wonder & Curiosity (The Physical Realm) and ending with Secret Garden (The Influence Realm).

However, there's another way you can begin exploring - by choosing the Realm you need most right now in your life. Here are some suggestions of beautiful inquiries you might ask to unearth this bit of wisdom:

Which of the Four Realms are you immediately drawn to? What do you need more of that you might be missing in your life at the moment?

Are you battling inertia and listlessness and wish you could energize yourself enough to go for a walk outdoors?
Start with: The Physical Realm Cards

Are you swimming in the same pool of inspiration online as everyone else, instead of exploring unique and original sources out in the real world?
Start with: The Influence Realm Cards

Are you feeling creatively stuck and in dire need of fresh ways to see and express?
Start with: The Creative Realm Cards

Are you feeling like you can barely hear yourself think most days, that it's been a long time since you were alone with your dreams and thoughts?

Start with: The Inner Realm Cards

Explorer Notes from Part I:

What have I learned from Part I?

PART II
Walking Into Wonder

Embark on a visual meditation.

Wonder & Curiosity

The Physical Realm

"**I** see things. Rabbits hopping in cumulus clouds. A wizened old man on a tree trunk. Dancing girls in pansy flowers."

Explorer's Notes

Pareidolia

*Pareidolia is seeing faces or scenes in unexpected places.
What can you spot today?*

I see things. Rabbits hopping in cumulus clouds. A wizened
old man on a tree trunk. Dancing girls in pansy flowers.
Pareidolia is a tendency to see figures and scenes in abstract
patterns or unexpected places, and it's one of my favorite
games to play on a wonder-walk. It encourages me to open my
eyes, look closer and interpret what I see beyond the literal.
It also stretches my imagination, hones my creative and visual
associations and transforms an ordinary walk into something
more interesting, meaningful and magical.

Interpretations:
Hidden messages
An optical illusion
An imagined perception
Clarity in vagueness
Meaning in the obscure or random

Realm Symbolism:
Wonder & Curiosity: The Physical Realm
Corresponding Symbolism: Earth, Materiality, Sensation
Ask: How does a 'Pareidolia' walk engage your senses?

Observe This on Your Wonder-Walk:

As you walk, pay attention to the textures and patterns on a
rock, in the sand or on tree trunks. Look closely at flowers
and leaves. Soften your gaze, relax and let your mind wander.

Observe your surroundings from all angles. Turn your
head, look at things from the corner of your eye, allow your
imagination to fly. Ask playful questions and practice drawing
unexpected associations: what does this rock look like? What
does this piece of seaweed make me think of?

Stop to inspect unusual markings for their pareidolia
potential. Be five years old again.

Activities to Try:

⊙ A Pareidolia Walk: On your next wonder-walk, look out for pareidolia in your surroundings by paying close attention. As soon as you spot one, write in your journal or notebook what you imagine you're seeing. Have fun with this. Invent a story, imagine a scenario, create your own personal fairy tale about how this image came to be. It might take you a few walks to see something interesting. Keep trying!
Tip: relax your mind, try not to overthink it. Being playful and whimsical helps.

⊙ Creative Pareidolia: Expand your pareidolia sightings into a creative project. Can you turn an interesting image into a series of surrealist paintings? An unusual collection of faces in fruit seeds? A soft toy collection of cloud animals? Let your imagination run wild, be playful and experimental!

Buzzing with ideas or enjoyed a 'Pareidolia' activity recently? Record them below:

Journal This:

What pareidolia did you experience? Describe what you saw.

Was it unexpected in any way? How did it happen?

Were there any stories and themes that emerged around your imaginings?

> **Explorer's Notes**

Related Cards:

How can you pair these related cards for a more interesting 'Pareidolia' wonder-walk?

Synesthesia, Connect, Pretend, Shape

> **Explorer's Notes**

"The invisible door to the otherworld hides in plain sight."

Explorer's Notes

Fairy Worlds

Imagine magical fairy worlds in your nature encounters.
What would your child-like wonder unveil?

When I was a girl, all treetops led to faraway lands, shuttered windows opened out to enchanted kingdoms, and forests were full of mysterious, magic folk. Every walk was a suspension of disbelief, an adventure steeped in imagination and fantasy. It infused a sheltered childhood in a tiny town with much splendor and marvel. As I grew up I realized that seeing fairy worlds in the everyday isn't the exclusive province of children - the invisible door to the otherworld hides in plain sight, we have only to open our hearts and minds to see it.

Interpretations:
Otherworld beyond five senses
A parallel reality
An enchanted or magical land
As pertaining to the Faerie
A fantasy or imagined world

Realm Symbolism:
Wonder & Curiosity: The Physical Realm
Corresponding Symbolism: Earth, Materiality, Sensation
Ask: How does a 'Fairy Worlds' walk engage your senses?

Observe This on Your Wonder-Walk:

Notice when the world around you resemble scenes from a fairy otherworld - floating islands in the middle of a pond like strange lands from a magical tale. A forest of giant redwood trees with its carpet of sorrel and moss like an accidental wandering into an elven kingdom.

Notice when your imagination begins to wander child-like, it's a sign that the land is inviting you to enter a world of the fantastical, the alternate, the magical.

Suspend disbelief, sharpen your senses for traces of enchantment: castles on foggy hills, mushroom rings, fields of spun gold, secret doorways, an ominous murder of crows.

Activities to Try:

- The Fairy Tale Walk: Plan a wonder-walk or a day's adventure around your favorite fairy-story. *Does it take place in the woods like "Hansel & Gretel" or "Little Red Riding Hood?" Rolling green hills? Gingerbread houses? Medieval towns with cobblestone streets?* Savor the experience, unleash your imagination and allow the story to unfold along your journey and enchant you. Create your own fairy tale if feeling inspired.

- Fairy Houses: Build a fairy house out of organic materials and leave it out in nature for fellow wonder-walkers to find. A good book to inspire ideas is <u>Fairy Houses: How to Create Whimsical Homes for Fairy Folk</u> by Sally J. Smith.

- Imagining Fairy Worlds: Build or bring along a few props on your wonder-walks: *a miniature toy animal - a rabbit, a deer, a little fairy house, miniature garden table and tea set, a toy car or carriage, little ceramic mushrooms, etc.* Set it up in nature, among flowers, in mossy banks, on tree branches. It helps you imagine yourself in otherworldly settings. Capture it on camera, journal or paint the scene. Also see the 'Thumbelina' card activities for more ideas.

Buzzing with ideas or enjoyed a 'Fairy Worlds' activity recently? Record them below:

Journal This:

What fairy stories do the places on your walk belong to? Why?

What scenes and settings on your walks are most likely to appear like magical fairy worlds?

How does it feel to imagine the Faerie in your everyday life?

What was your favorite fairy tale as a child? Describe the setting, characters and storyline. Why do you think it resonated?

Explorer's Notes

Related Cards:

How can you pair these related cards for a more interesting 'Fairy Worlds' wonder-walk?

Portals, The Woods, Story, Thumbelina

Explorer's Notes

"How can we understand and engage the plants around us with our heart and senses?"

Explorer's Notes

Flora

The world of flora is beyond the flamboyant.
Observe where, when and why they bloom.

Leaves, flowers, tendrils, roots, buds, twigs.
Flora is both the living world of plants that share the land
we belong to, and the goddess of flowers, nature, and spring
time. Flora sustains and protects the earth. It is life-giving and
life-affirming, and we are its stewards in the circle of life. This
card invites to ponder our relationship with the plant kingdom,
to consider these lively creatures that beat to a slower drum,
worthy of our fascination. How can we understand and engage
the plants around us with our heart and senses? What gifts of
flora should we celebrate and appreciate?

Interpretations:
Native or indigenous plant life
Greenery or vegetation
Of flowers and blooms
Roman goddess of flowers

Realm Symbolism:
Wonder & Curiosity: The Physical Realm
Corresponding Symbolism: Earth, Materiality, Sensation
Ask: How does a 'Flora' walk engage your senses?

Observe This on Your Wonder-Walk:

As you walk, notice how the plants around you move, albeit at
a much slower pace. Observe how tendrils circle and cockscrew
around the fence, how sunflowers angle their heads toward the
sun, how the roots of a tree spread away from its trunk.

Notice the wondrous gifts of plants - their fruits, flowers,
seeds and the many shapes, colors and forms they come in. Pay
attention to the scents of flora all around you- wild rosemary,
sagebrush, eucalyptus. What else can you smell?

Observe how plants react to changes in the temperature,
sunlight and humidity around them. What flowers open in the
morning and closes at night? What is the texture of an aspen
bark? Which plants are native, and which invasive?

Activities to Try:

⊙ Flora Habitats: Over the next two weeks, walk the natural plant habitats around you to observe the types of plants that thrive in that area. *E.g. wetlands, forests, estuaries, chaparral, grasslands.* Sketch the general growth patterns: *E.g. coastal oaks and ferns in the forests and woodlands, eelgrass in the wetlands, sea figs in the dunes.*
-iNaturalist is a great phone app to help you identify plants in a mapped area.
-Creative challenge: Create a colorful watercolor map of the plant habitats in your area and draw in the native flora found in them.

⊙ Native Flora Walk: Head out on a wonder-walk to study and celebrate the native plants around you. Alternatively, visit a nearby botanical garden, preferably one with native plants from foreign lands. Refer to the previous page on walking observations. Engage with the plants you encounter and journal your discoveries afterward.

⊙ Gifts from Nature: This is a fun activity for connecting to native plants and their gifts (always check with your local state or national park about bringing home 'gifts' from nature). Choose one of these activities to try out. *Pressed flowers, plant curio cabinet, natural plant-based crafts, botanical illustration, foraging plants for food, mandalas.*

Buzzing with ideas or enjoyed a 'Flora' activity recently? Record them below:

Journal This:

What is your favorite native plant where you live? Why?

If you were a tree, which tree would you be? Why?

What are some ways you enjoy engaging with plants?

How can you improve your relationship with the plant kingdom? Describe 3 ideas or actions you'll implement.

Explorer's Notes

Related Cards:

How can you pair these related cards for a more interesting 'Flora' wonder-walk?

Dusk, Height, Edges, Study

Explorer's Notes

"No matter where I am, I often find myself unconsciously seeking the highest places to be in, the physical craving for freedom and perspective, bone-deep."

Explorer's Notes

Height

A hilltop view is sacrosanct in many landscapes.
What will you learn of the land when you gain height?

My love for high places have long roots. Growing up, we always
lived on hills because my dad loved having a commanding
view of the land around and feeling free as a bird when he
stepped outside. Indirectly he was teaching me to always rise
up and look at the big picture in life and it has served me very
well. This card was painted perched high up on a cliff by the
ocean, a view of the blue waters and the wooded shoreline as
far as the eye could see. No matter where I am, I often find
myself unconsciously seeking the highest places to be in, the
physical craving for freedom and perspective, bone-deep.

Interpretations:
Rising up above all.
An unobstructed view.
The big picture or perspective,
Being in command.
Freedom.

Realm Symbolism:
Wonder & Curiosity: The Physical Realm
Corresponding Symbolism: Earth, Materiality, Sensation
Ask: How does a 'Height' walk engage your senses?

Observe This on Your Wonder-Walk:

In difficult landscapes (like deserts and rainforests), gaining
height is the only way to get a lay of the land and how to
proceed if uncertain. Look around you. Where can you climb
to if you've lost your way?

How many feet/meters above sea level are you? How can you
find out? Is there any evidence that this used to be under the
ocean? Are you finding seashells on top of mountains?

How did this place (man-made or natural) become the highest
point in the area? What happened through time?

Activities to Try:

⊙ Top of the World: Plan a day's adventure to the highest landmark in your town or county. Learn about why it was built on such high ground. Pack a picnic, bring your journal. Take wonder-walks and journal or paint what the original occupants would have felt and seen.

⊙ Read up on famous monuments and places in history where height is an important part of its feature: *the Tor in Glastonbury, hilltowns in Tuscany or the Angkor Wat in Cambodia.* What are some of the pragmatic, spiritual or cultural reasons for being high up?

⊙ Height Survival: Imagine another time when access to height would have meant life or death. *A tower in a time of war? Knowledge gained of animals grazing in the distance? The best valley to grow food?* Visit these places (if possible) to understand what would have been at stake.

Buzzing with ideas or enjoyed a 'Height' activity recently? Record them below:

Journal This:

How does being high up make you feel? Describe vividly how your senses were engaged and what emotions arose.

What are some areas in your life that you wish you could climb up and have a bigger perspective of, right now?

What are some of your favorite places for unobstructed views? What do you like most about them?

Explorer's Notes

Related Cards:

How can you pair these related cards for a more interesting 'Height' wonder-walk?

Discomfort, Belonging, Journey, Hidden

Explorer's Notes

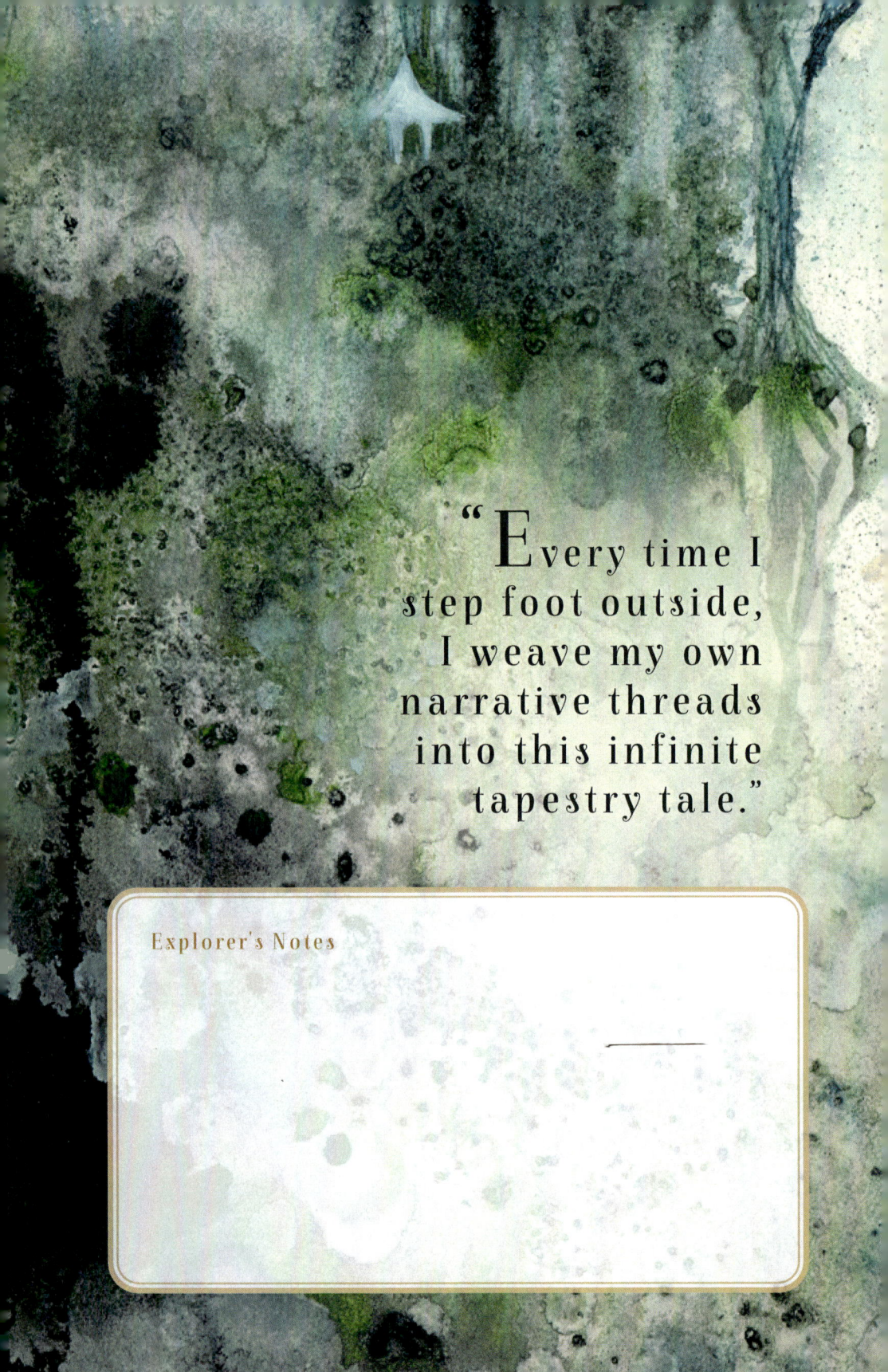

"Every time I step foot outside, I weave my own narrative threads into this infinite tapestry tale."

Explorer's Notes

Story

*What stories, real or imagined, can you weave
about what you're seeing?*

The land pulses with the stories of its inhabitants, past, present
and future. Every time I step foot outside, I weave my own
narrative threads into this infinite tapestry tale. In the past,
before we learned to read and write and live disconnected from
our environments, we told, sang and danced stories of our lands
to remember how much we depended on it for our survival.
We told the story of plants, of wildlife, of the celestial skies,
and we told magical tales of enchanted beasts, and journeys
to faraway realms. This card invites us to remember a lost time
when our stories intertwine intimately with the land's, and what
reconnecting in such a way again would mean to us.

Interpretations:
Folk tales, stories of a people and their lands
Myth-making; songlines,
History, legend or narrative
Allegory, fairy tale or fable

Realm Symbolism:
Wonder & Curiosity: The Physical Realm
Corresponding Symbolism: Earth, Materiality, Sensation
Ask: How does a 'Story' walk engage your senses?

Observe This on Your Wonder-Walk:

The purpose of a 'storied' wonder-walk is to observe if narratives
make your walks more wonderous and engaging. Would a
place be more memorable if you spun a tale around what you
encounter? Would you connect deeper with a place or a walk if
you knew more about how it came to be?

Observe if anything on your walk reminds you of fairy tales,
myths or urban legends you might have heard in childhood or
since? Notice if you intuitively associate any physical elements
in your environment with a fairy tale, like the woods with
"Hansel and Gretel", rolling hills with Lord of the Rings. Observe
when a place ignites a sense of curiosity for its many tales.

Activities to Try:

⊙ A Storybook Walk: Explore a walk inspired by your favorite storybook. *Spend a day picnicking and exploring caves like your favorite adventure books, find your very own <u>Secret Garden</u> or <u>Alice in Wonderland</u> experiences where you live, or explore your own version of Middle Earth or Mordor.*
-Alternatively, arrange for a trip to a dream location that feels right out of a storybook: *a medieval town, a castle, misty mountains, etc.*
-Ponder how the story influences the walking experience. What do you notice more, or less? Is there a blurred line between fantasy and reality?

⊙ Heritage Site Adventure: Plan a dream adventure to a famous cultural or world heritage site. Stay with the locals, immerse yourself in their rituals, beliefs, and culture. Get familiar with their history and mythology at a local musuem. Observe how story-immersion colors your experience of the place. Are your senses more attuned to your surroundings? Is your imagination fired up? Journal your feelings and discoveries.

⊙ A Storied Walk: Research your favorite place to walk where you live at the local library or natural history museum. Look up old maps and photographs to reference how it used to look. Pay attention to stories about past inhabitants, as well as myths and folktales told about the place. Take your usual wonder-walk. How has it changed your experience of the place? What are you more sensitive to? Journal your feelings, thoughts and discoveries.

Buzzing with ideas or enjoyed a 'Story' activity recently? Record them below:

Journal This:

What stories, myths or folktales come up often for you on your walks? What do you think you're meant to learn?

What storybook or mythical places do you often imagine your walks taking place in? Why do you think you're drawn to imagining these dream places?

Does learning about the myth, folklore or history behind a place changes the way you experience it?

Explorer's Notes

Related Cards:

How can you pair these related cards for a more interesting 'Story' wonder-walk?

Journey, Roots, Connect, Symbolism

Explorer's Notes

"It's the medicinal dose of different in the lullabying cocoon of everyday life."

Explorer's Notes

Disruption

If you disrupted your usual route, what new and extraordinary things will you see?

Disruption jolts us out of complacency like a thunderstorm on a lazy summer day. Disruption is a ripple, a tear, a wrinkle in the smooth fabric of routine. It's the medicinal dose of different in the lullabying cocoon of everyday life, the perfect prescription for creative apathy. Disruption shakes things up, makes room for chaos and happenstance, for the messy and unplanned, for the new and fresh. This card invites us to step off the beaten path, to be comfortable with uncertainty, and to allow for magic outside the ordinary.

Interpretations:
To shake things up
Off the beaten path, outside the ordinary
Comfort in uncertainty
Thinking outside the box
Chaos, upheaval, havoc

Realm Symbolism:
Wonder & Curiosity: The Physical Realm
Corresponding Symbolism: Earth, Materiality, Sensation
Ask: How can we 'disrupt' our walk?

Observe This on Your Wonder-Walk:

Take the road less traveled today. Choose a new trail, leave the map at home, get lost if you're a planner. Dip your toe in the river or the ocean if you've never done so before. If you often take the uphill path, choose a downhill one. Hop on a bus and stop in the middle of nowhere to wander and explore.

What do you notice when you disrupt your walk? Are your surroundings more interesting when seen from a different angle? Do you notice more because it's all new? Observe if your senses become more alert when experiencing something outside of routine. Is it uncomfortable or enjoyable?

What is clearer, brighter, more vivid? What smells and sounds are you noticing that eluded you before?

Activities to Try:

⊙ **The Creative Adventure:** Plan a weekend creative adventure to a nearby town for at least a few hours to shake things up and awaken the senses. Try new restaurants, walk in new parks, visit the museums. You have permission to explore to your heart's content. Observe what you notice, if it feels different, and what feelings and creative ideas are emerging from this adventure?

⊙ **The Friend Walk:** Invite a friend or a family member on a wonder-walk with you at your regular spot if you normally walk solo. Introduce him or her to your favorite sights and activities. Observe your friend's reactions, notice what he or she does differently from you. Experience the surroundings through their eyes. Journal how it feels to wonder-walk with someone else. Did you notice anything new or different? What did you enjoy about it?

⊙ **The Experimental Walk:** Was the effort worth the hard work? *What would your walk be like if you wore a costume, skipped, hopped or waved hello to everyone you pass? What if you brought your guitar along and stopped to play it every so often?* Experiment with trying something eccentric, whimsical or unexpected on your walks and observe what happens. How do people interact with you and does it change your walking experience? Journal your findings.

Buzzing with ideas or enjoyed a 'Disruption' activity recently? Record them below:

Journal This:

Why am I drawn to a little disruption right now?

What are some ways I can disrupt my everyday walks (and life)? Braindump.

What was the most satisfying thing about my 'disruption' today?

What enjoyable experience would I have missed had I not disrupted my walk today?

> Explorer's Notes

Related Cards:

How can you pair these related cards for a more interesting 'Disruption' wonder-walk?

Discomfort, Follow the Rabbit, Edges, Play

> Explorer's Notes

"I heard a distinct birdsong and immediately pictured a twinkling, starry night sky."

Explorer's Notes

Synesthesia

*Synesthesia is the practice of merging your senses.
Can you relate two senses today?*

One of my most vivid synesthesia experiences was during
a wonder-walk in town. I heard a distinct birdsong and
immediately pictured a twinkling, starry night sky. While I am
not a true synesthete, this experience gave me a glimpse into
the wondrous world of sense-blending. Synesthesia is the rare
and unusual connection of two senses, a natural phenomenon.
To me, it is poetry embodied, like sounds have colors or words
have smells and both senses are experienced interchangeably.
This card invites us to explore combining our senses and
experiences, to see if it would make our walks and adventures
more enchanting and memorable.

Interpretations:
Rising up above all.
An unobstructed view.
The big picture or perspective,
Being in command.
Freedom.

Realm Symbolism:
Wonder & Curiosity: The Physical Realm
Corresponding Symbolism: Earth, Materiality, Sensation
Ask: How does a 'Synesthesia' walk engage your senses?

Observe This on Your Wonder-Walk:

Notice if you have any hidden synesthetic gifts? Does the
sound of a foghorn make you think of the color blue? Is the
smell of pine leaves velvety to touch?

As you walk, notice if any senses are relating to each other
in unexpected ways. Even if like me, you aren't a natural
synesthete, try to form associations between your emotions,
senses and thoughts to remember the experience more vividly.

The more you can involve all five senses in a particular event,
the more it will leave an impression, and the more visceral the
recollection later on.

Activities to Try:

⊙ Color & Sound: The next time you're on a walk, experiment with associating colors with sounds. Listen out for sounds of natural elements, of the plants and creatures in the environment around you. Think of what colors the sounds remind you of. *The foghorn is a misty blue-gray. Sparrows chirping in bursts of lemon-yellow. The roar of the ocean recalls stormy hues of indigo.* Assign a color if nothing comes to mind. Practice this regularly and observe if your brain begins to make automatic associations.

⊙ Color & Taste: In this variation, experiment with imagining what the colors you see on your walk would taste like. Explore wild and unusual combinations, try selecting elements that don't ordinarily go together. Be intuitive and lighthearted; don't overthink this. *The rosy pink of the sunset tastes like raspberry popsicle. The inky night sky tastes like a crisp sheet of nori. The limestone cliffs like vanilla cake.* Observe where your associations come from, if you can trace the origins.

⊙ Explore the use of synesthesia in literature as inspiration for your wonder-walks. *I smell trouble. Bitter cold. Symphony of color.* Read the wonderful book The Phantom Tollbooth, whose author Norton Juster is a synesthete. How many examples of synesthesia can you find in this book?

Buzzing with ideas or enjoyed a 'Synesthesia' activity recently? Record them below:

Journal This:

What everyday memories would you like to recall more vividly? Can you explore synesthesia to help with this?

What kind of associations would allow you to remember your walks and adventures more viscerally? Are you drawn to pairing sights with colors? Sounds with feelings? What would you be excited to blend?

What specific scenarios on your walks or adventures do you find particularly intriguing as a synesthetic experiment?

Explorer's Notes

Related Cards:

How can you pair these related cards for a more interesting 'Synesthesia' wonder-walk?

Memory, Connect, Poetry, Color

Explorer's Notes

"**D**iscomfort is a two-sided coin, strife on one, aliveness on the other."

Explorer's Notes

Discomfort

Brave discomfort on your Walk today.
What happens if you climb higher or feel the dark?

There is incredible glory and beauty on the other side of discomfort. It's where we find ourselves, discover what we're made of. It's that magnificent sunset photo made possible by the mountain we had to scale, staying later, waking up earlier, going where no one dared. It's a freezing but breathtaking open water swim at daybreak amidst the herons, or the triumphant oversized painting that took 6 months to paint. Discomfort is a two-sided coin, strife on one, aliveness on the other. This card invites us to step outside our cozy bubbles of contentment to ask: what untold wonders await us beyond our perceived limits?

Interpretations:
Stepping outside our comfort zone
Pushing our limits, challenging ourselves
Hardship, displeasure, uneasiness, mild pain
Doing the difficult thing

Realm Symbolism:
Wonder & Curiosity: The Physical Realm
Corresponding Symbolism: Earth, Materiality, Sensation
Ask: How does a 'Discomfort' walk engage your senses?

Observe This on Your Wonder-Walk:

As you walk, examine your fears: are you afraid of heights? Does standing at the edge of the cliff looking down at the 100-foot drop break you out in goosebumps?

Are you afraid of walking through a forest in the dark? Are there places that bring up unpleasant memories? What makes your skin crawl? Observe what feels like too much work. Is it that strenuous climb up that steep hill? Taking the long way around the lake? Notice how it feels if you (safely) faced your worries, fears and displeasure, and did it anyway.

How does it feel to push past your discomfort on a walk? What feelings, emotions or thoughts are coming up?
Do you feel more alive?

Activities to Try:

⊙ A Walking Challenge: Plan a walk that makes you slightly uncomfortable. Bring a journal and sketch/ paint how it makes you feel. *Climb a hill in your area, tough it out even when your legs begin to burn. Appreciate the view on top of that hill. If the dark gives you the shivers, get a friend to join you for a midnight walk on a full moon night. If you often sleep in, wake up just before sunrise so you can experience the peaceful early morning. Go for a walk in the rain or snow - get wet and cold and uncomfortable and celebrate with a hot bath and cup of tea after.*

   Observe how you feel before, during and after the challenge. Did you experience anything interesting and new because of discomfort?

⊙ The Pot of Gold: Plan a weekend adventure with a high effort, high reward ratio, something you've always thought too difficult to attempt. *A tough hike that culminates with a magical hidden waterfall. A long bike ride into town for afternoon tea. Amazing sea caves accessible only by a challenging kayak trip.*

   Take a beautiful photograph to celebrate your 'pot of gold' at the end of your hard work. Rejoice at pushing past your discomfort to experience something so special. Journal how it feels to take on this adventure. Was the effort worth the hard work?

Buzzing with ideas or enjoyed a 'Discomfort' activity recently? Record them below:

Journal This:

What feels uncomfortable for you outdoors? What scares you or feels like too much effort? What do you think you can't possibly do?

How do you feel once you've pushed through the discomfort? Describe your feelings and emotions in detail.

If you can choose one discomfort to take on right now, what would it be? Why is it important to you?

Explorer's Notes

Related Cards:

How can you pair these related cards for a more interesting 'Discomfort' wonder-walk?

Height, Darkness, Discernment, Disruption

Explorer's Notes

"It is the ability to observe, see and make meaning from the seemingly trivial details that appear along our journey's paths."

Landmark

Look out for landmarks. What do they tell you about the land and its inhabitants?

All my life I was conditioned to remember landmarks, whether natural or man-made, as prominent features of my environments. But landmarks are more than easily recognizable guideposts of history, place and culture. They are a part of a remarkable wayfaring system stretching back to primitive times. This includes the ability to observe, see and make meaning from the seemingly trivial details that appear along our journey's paths. This card invites us to not only examine landmarks as tools of navigation, but also to observe what it might mean to our personal stories when we notice something over another.

Interpretations:
Marks and signs on a journey's path
Places of interest; memorable places
A system of wayfaring; guideposts
Distinguishing features of the environment

Realm Symbolism:
Wonder & Curiosity: The Physical Realm
Corresponding Symbolism: Earth, Materiality, Sensation
Ask: What 'Landmarks' can you spot on your walks?

Observe This on Your Wonder-Walk:

What distinguishing features of your surroundings do you notice around you as you walk? What do you automatically assign as landmarks? The smokestack noticeable from 3 miles away? Or the moss-covered rock by your foot?

Notice if landmarks are permanent or ephemeral to you. Observe if you pay attention to less-prominent landmarks. If you didn't know your way around, can you navigate your way to your destination? Can you remember these guideposts if you reverse your journey in the direction you came from?

Can you guess what the landmarks you noticed communicate about the place, its inhabitants and the local way of life?

Activities to Try:

⊙ Landmark Memories: This is one of my favorite journaling exercises, inspired by Hannah Hinchman's method for memory-walking.
-Start with the memory of a recent place you've visited on a trip, or from your hometown or favorite place as a child.
-Close your eyes and imagine yourself back in this place. Once you have a clear picture, map out the landmarks you remember as clearly as you can.
-Journal why these were prominent to you, what they signify or symbolize for that memory or journey.

⊙ A Primitive Wayfaring Journey: Plan a quick (and safe) walking journey in a place you're unfamiliar with where you'll be returning the same way you came. *It could be a short stroll in an unfamiliar part of town, or a new trail you haven't hiked before.* You'll be navigating this journey without any modern instruments or maps.
-.Make a note of all the landmarks, prominent or less so, along your journey.
-Observe the character of these landmarks - *e.g. permanent, ephemeral, shape, color, natural, etc.*
-Memorize these landmarks so that you'll remember them in the reverse direction.
-How easy is it to find your way? What was difficult? What would make it easier?

Buzzing with ideas or enjoyed a 'Landmark' activity recently? Record them below:

Journal This:

What are some of the distinguishing landmarks around where you live or walk? What are some of the less prominent ones?

What makes a landmark memorable to you? What if any, personal significance does it have for you?

How do you think these landmarks are significant to your community beyond navigational purposes?

Explorer's Notes

Related Cards:

How can you pair these related cards for a more interesting 'Landmark' wonder-walk?

Journey, Memory, Belonging, Shape

Explorer's Notes

"How have we anchored ourselves to our environments through our journey stories?"

Explorer's Notes

Roots

Roots are hidden anchors.
How many natural ways of anchoring can you spot?

Just as the roots of a tree spread out in a complex hidden network
underground, so much of our origins are embedded deep within
the memories - ours and our ancestors' - that interwine the
land we belong to. This card invites us to ponder: how have we
anchored ourselves to our environments through our journey
stories? What flashes of the strangely familiar in our everyday
can we trace back to our buried depths? How can we celebrate and
nourish this precious wellspring of our very being and aliveness?

Interpretations:
To establish deeply, implanted
Anchoring, moored, make port
Origin, heritage, lineage
Hidden depths, unseen source
A belonging, acclimatization, adaptation

Realm Symbolism:
Wonder & Curiosity: The Physical Realm
Corresponding Symbolism: Earth, Materiality, Sensation
Ask: How does a 'Roots' walk engage your senses?

Observe This on Your Wonder-Walk:

Study the visible roots of trees and plants around you on your
walks. What do they reveal about the tree or plant? Observe when
a plant is in drought, its roots not receiving enough water or
nourishment. How does it look? What other interesting ways do
plants anchor themselves for nourishment?

Can you spot the different types of roots? The aerial roots
of vines, strangler figs and spider plants? The stilt roots of
mangroves? What about symbiotic plants that live on other trees?
Where do their roots go? What do you find most fascinting?

What parallels can you draw between the roots you see in nature
and the idea of rooting as an inhabitant of the land?

Activities to Try:

○ Reconnecting to Your Roots: Plan a wonder-walk or adventure to a place that reconnects you with your roots, i.e. your cultural heritage, education, ancestry, lineage, etc. *It could be a visit to a museum, dining at a restaurant that serves the food of your ancestors, or visiting a cultural fair, show or event honoring your heritage.*
-Did you learn anything interesting or surprising about your origins?
-How did it feel to reconnect to your roots?

○ A Rooting Adventure: If possible, plan a trip to your hometown or a place where you spent most of your childhood. It could be your grandparents' home, a place where you lived for many years, or somewhere you connected with and rooted deeply.
-Take a walk on a fondly remembered street. Visit the places you spent lots of time. Talk to your grandparents about how times were like when they were young.
With fresh eyes, what elements of the land, culture and community shaped who you are right now?
- What are some ways you rooted in this environment? How you are changed from it?

○ A Botanical Adventure: Visit a botanical garden or conservatory in your area or neighboring town to study the roots of trees or plants not native to your area. Sketch, journal or photograph your findings. What did you find fascinating? What did you learn?

Buzzing with ideas or enjoyed a 'Roots' activity recently? Record them below:

Journal This:

What roots did you notice on your walk? What was most fasinating about them?

What does roots and rooting mean to you? How can you relate the biology of a tree or plant to how you've established life where you are right now?

Are you neglecting your roots? Journal some ways reconnecting to your roots would nourish you right now.

Explorer's Notes

Related Cards:

How can you pair these related cards for a more interesting 'Roots' wonder-walk?

Hidden, Home, Journey, Belonging

Explorer's Notes

"**S**ometimes we look, we see, we examine, but we do not notice."

Explorer's Notes

Notice

Notice, not just see.
What can you observe without judgment?

To notice is to relax into observation. To let intuition, our
senses, and the deep unconscious guide what we experience in
the moment. Noticing is a meditation, a quiet viewing detached
from the mind. Sometimes we look, we see, we examine, but
we do not notice. This card invites us to run our eyes over our
surroundings and consider without expectation and judgment.
Dust motes glittering like fairy dust. Sun rays streaming through
the window. The croaking of frogs after a rainstorm. What have
we missed when we were busy looking?

Interpretations:
To consider, pay attention to
To see without expectation or judgement
To become aware of something
Mindful observation

Realm Symbolism:
Wonder & Curiosity: The Physical Realm
Corresponding Symbolism: Earth, Materiality, Sensation
Ask: What do you 'Notice' on your walk?

Observe This on Your Wonder-Walk:

As you walk, release all emotions, pre-conceived notions,
expectations, or judgments about what you should be seeing
around you. Allow yourself to embark on a visual meditation
instead. Softly recite what you're seeing if it helps, you'd be
surprised at how sensuous and present it makes the experience.

What catches your eye? Is it sea foam tumbling across a sandy
beach? Or vultures circling in a cloudless sky? There is no right
and wrong to noticing. Observe the bigger picture with sweeping
eyes, or carefully study the microcosm under a rock. Delight
in the non-knowing and non-analyzing of what you're seeing.
Rejoice in a simple, mindful looking.

Lastly, notice what you notice. Pay attention to what tugs at your
senses in the moment. Perceive, but resist drawing conclusions.

Activities to Try:

⊙ A Walking Meditation: Plan for a meditative wonder-walk somewhere peaceful for your first attempt. Release all expectations of 'going somewhere' or 'seeing something'.
-Begin with a reverence and gratitude for being able to step foot on the land and in the sea.
-Take each step mindfully, paying attention to what you see around you. Pull yourself back to the present moment if your mind starts to wander.
-With each slow, deliberate step, draw a deep breath and feel yourself being grounded to the earth. Celebrate being alive at this moment for the big and little things in life.

⊙ Creative Expression with Noticing: Pick a favorite medium for your next walk, it could be watercolors, pencil sketching, photography or poetry-writing.
-Get comfortable and free-paint, free-write or free-sketch the first thing you noticed that caught your attention.
-Challenge yourself to work loosely and quickly, without letting your conscious mind take over.

Buzzing with ideas or enjoyed a 'Notice' activity recently? Record them below:

Journal This:

What did you notice on your walk today? Did anything stand out in particular? Describe the experience.

What was the first thing that drew your attention?

Have you ever found yourself looking too hard and stuck in your head when you walk? How does it feel to just notice and be present in the moment?

Explorer's Notes

Related Cards:

How can you pair these related cards for a more interesting 'Notice' wonder-walk?

Naiveté, Listen, Mood Painting, Immersion

Explorer's Notes

"It's laying down roots, surrounding ourselves with the other, dissolving boundaries."

Explorer's Notes

Belonging

How do we belong here?
What are the physical evidences that we are a part of all this?

Belonging is the yearning to be a part of something - of being one with the land, a community, culture, heritage. It's laying down roots, surrounding ourselves with the other, dissolving boundaries. Belonging is the act of knowing, loving, mapping the exterior with our soul and senses. Having moved multiple times since childhood, this card invites me to explore my relationship with the places I call home and ponder: how can I participate in my surroundings? What can I do to engage, attach and anchor myself to the land?

Interpretations:
Being a part of something; assimilating
To have a relationship with; form attachment to
To participate in or engage deeper with
Reuniting, returning to the source, anchoring
Living in, inhabiting, residing

Realm Symbolism:
Wonder & Curiosity: The Physical Realm
Corresponding Symbolism: Earth, Materiality, Sensation
Ask: How can you 'Belong' to this land with all your senses?

Observe This on Your Wonder-Walk:

Walk as if the land means something to you, either as an outsider looking in longingly, or a local resident filled with love for your home turf. Notice specific features of the land you feel most connected to, that familiar sense of coming home. Conversely, does anything make you feel like an outsider?

Look out for that melancholic tug of yearning to be a part of your environment in a deeper way. Ponder how you can be a more intimate participant within it - can you rename your favorite places, weave them into your own journey, walk or ride it everyday? Would it help to volunteer for the state park, join an urban planting group or attend a county state fair?

What stories of the land can you weave into your own?

Activities to Try:

⊙ Local for a Day: Spend a day in town or a favorite place where you live. Sink in, immerse, do all the fun and unique things that make you feel like part of a community - *local breweries, eateries and music venues, shop at a farmers market, check out the local artisans, volunteer at an event*
-Alternate Adventure: Do this any time you visit a new place. Go out of your way to experience a place like a local. Book a room in a local neighborhood. Opt to visit local recommendations over tourist destinations. Spend a few days 'belonging' somewhere else.
-Journal how it feels to 'belong' to a place, a community, a culture or heritage not your own.

⊙ Land Participation: How can you create an ongoing relationship with the place where you live? Select one of these activities to explore, feel free to add to this list as you begin 'belonging' on your own:
-Choose an activity a week from other card chapters in this Explorer's Journal.
-Volunteer with a local nature group - *state parks, local parks, land conservation, etc.*
-Sign up for a local Naturalist course near you to learn about the native wildlife and habitats.
-Read up about history of the area at the library or join a local historical society.
-Start a creative project inspired by your surroundings - *make a fun short film, create a painting or photo series, write a story or a poem, etc.*

Buzzing with ideas or enjoyed a 'Belonging' activity recently? Record them below:

Journal This:

What do I feel most connected to where I live right now? Why?

How and why do I belong to this place and vice versa? What have I done so far to root deeper in my home environment?

What and where do I want to belong to but still feel like an outsider? Why is that so?

How can I reconnect with this land I call home, and its community, culture or heritage?

Explorer's Notes

Related Cards:

How can you pair these related cards for a more interesting 'Belonging' wonder-walk?

Roots, Home, Connection, Immersion

Explorer's Notes

Notice what the world inspires in your creative heart.

Magic-Making

The Creative Realm

"Perhaps it's the bright red sun sinking as it stains everything a juicy tint of red and pink, leaving you speechless and mesmerized."

Explorer's Notes

First Love

Love at first sight. An always infatuation.
How will you express what captured your heart?

There is a magical moment that happens when I glimpse a
glorious sight on a walk for the first time, or through new eyes
from being long away. A sudden rush of feeling, a swelling
of the heart, a swooning breathlessness. Regardless if it's a
scarlet sunset or a canopy of mossy oaks that sweeps me off
my feet, my creative heart is eager to capture the ardor in
some form - a haiku, a mood painting, a perfectly framed
camera shot.

Interpretations:
Love at first sight.
An infatuation.
Reunited at last.
An old favorite.
Puppy love.

Realm Symbolism:
Magic-Making: The Creative Realm
Corresponding Symbolism: Fire, Passion, Intuition
Ask: How can you capture your 'First Love' walk?

Observe This on Your Wonder-Walk:

Notice what captures your heart immediately at the start of
your walk. Is it the fog rolling in, blanketing the forest in a
mystical, mysterious feeling?

Perhaps it's the bright red sun sinking as it stains everything
a juicy tint of red and pink, leaving you speechless and
mesmerized. Or it could be as subtle as the quietness that
settles over a park in the late evening, an immediate hush of
peace like a welcome hug.

Notice what it inspires in your creative heart. Is a poem on
the tip of your tongue? An itch to sketch the scene on paper?
Allow yourself to be lured by your Muse.

Activities to Try:

⊙ First Love Memories: Close your eyes and journey
   back to your favorite places in your childhood
   hometown or holiday trips. Can you see it
   vividly? On a piece of paper or in your journal,
   memory-walk (as inspired by Hannah Hinchman)
   these places and record them as you see them
   in your mind's eye. Observe what captures your
   attention. What do you remember fondly? *The
   old tree you and your best friend gossiped under?
   The bookstore in the hidden alley that you spent
   hours in?* Write all the details down and ponder:
   What are some of your environmental 'First
   Loves' from childhood? Draw, paint or write
   about your discoveries.

⊙ Rose-Tinted Places: Plan a day's adventure to
   your favorite haunts from childhood (or remind
   you of them, if you live far away). *A walk in
   strangely familiar woods, a seaside town of
   many playful summers past.* Soak in the rose-
   tinted memories and observe how it colors your
   experience in the moment. Photograph your
   fondest encounters in a way that tells a story.

Buzzing with ideas or enjoyed a 'First Love'
activity recently? Record them below:

Journal This:

What are some of your favorite nature encounters from childhood? Are you still drawn to the same scenes and experiences today?

How have these fond childhood encounters shaped your view of the natural (or built) world today?

What are you instantly drawn to on your current walks? Why?

Explorer's Notes

Related Cards:

How can you pair these related cards for a more interesting 'First Love' wonder-walk?

Memory, Roots, Naiveté, Belonging

Explorer's Notes

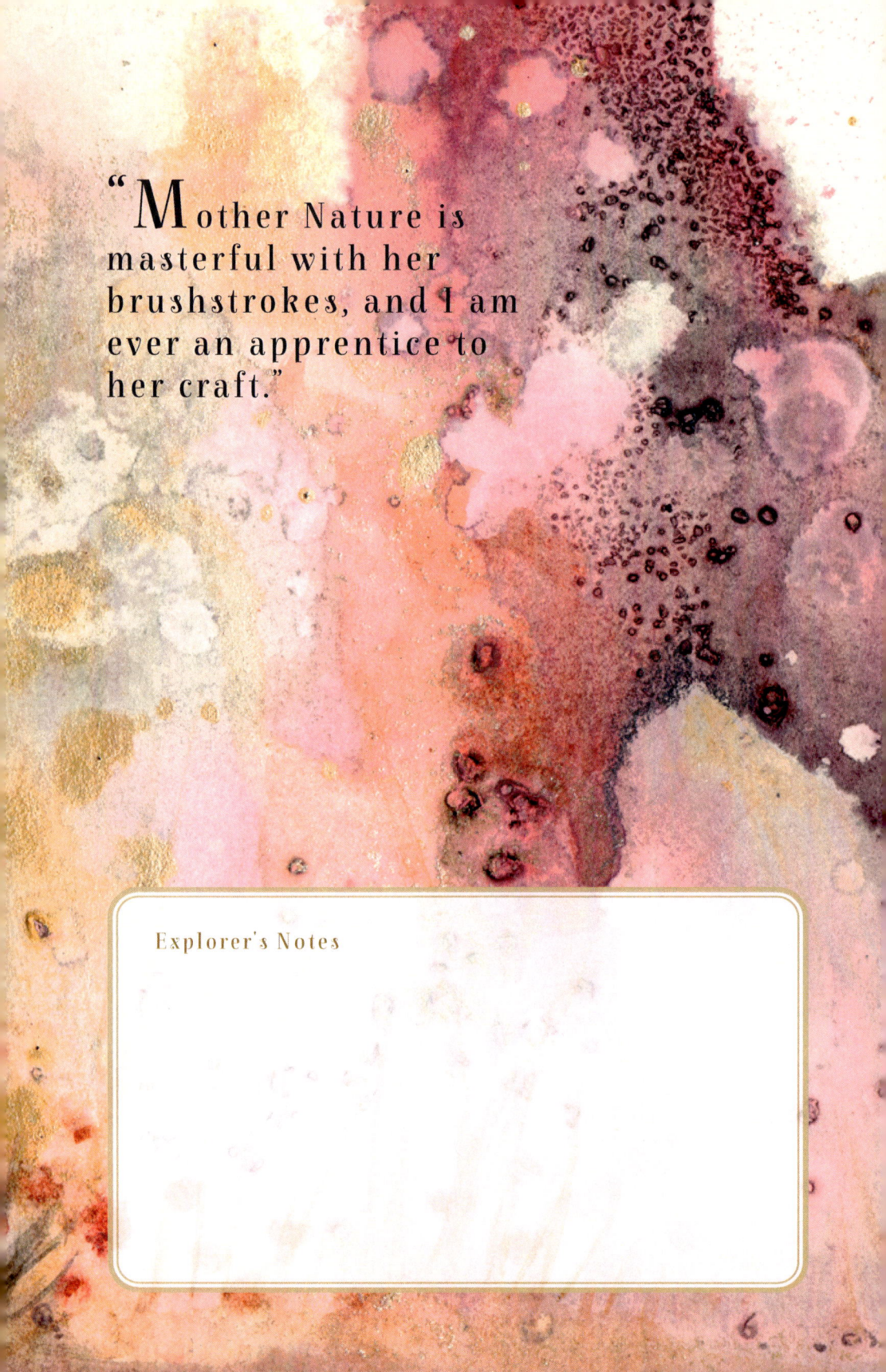

"Mother Nature is masterful with her brushstrokes, and I am ever an apprentice to her craft."

Explorer's Notes

Textures

*Course, medium or fine, textures abound in the landscape.
How can you capture tactility?*

A walk in nature is my favorite way to seek new textures, shapes and forms to enrich my paintings. There is enough exquisite detail all around if I remember to look closer and soften my gaze. The peeling bark of a eucalyptus tree, a sea of wildflowers like textured dots on an Impressionist painting, the striations and erosions in rocky tidepools.
Mother Nature is masterful with her brushstrokes, and I am ever an apprentice to her craft.

Interpretations:
Shape, geometry, forms
Patterns and marks, bumps and protrusions
Tactility, dimensionality
Traces left behind by weather or organisms

Realm Symbolism:
Magic-Making: The Creative Realm
Corresponding Symbolism: Fire, Passion, Intuition
Ask: How will you capture the 'Textures' from your walk?

Observe This on Your Wonder-Walk:

Look out patterns and textures that appear over and over again in nature: bubbles, waves, branches, fractures, fluids, grains. Are there places that have more of a certain type of pattern than others?

Notice similarities between patterns in organic and non-organic elements, between large-scale (*e.g.* shape of hills, rock striations, clouds) and small-scale forms (*e.g.* butterfly wings, leaf veins, sand grains).

Observe what textures are caused by forces of nature, i.e., the sun, wind, rain, snow, and what are caused by man or other organisms. Ponder if these patterns and textures remind you of something else - rock striations like layers of cake, the inside of abalone shells like shimmering lakes and rivers.

Activities to Try:

⊙ A Pattern Adventure: Put together your Creative Adventure Kit with a sketchbook and drawing, writing or painting implements (see Part 1 for ideas). Bring it along your walks and record the patterns and textures you see in nature: *e.g. spirals, bubbles, waves, branches, fractures, fluids, grains, etc.*
Where do these patterns and textures overlap in nature? Answer some of the questions from the previous page on wonder-walk observations.

⊙ Pattern Reads: Dig into these additional readings on shapes, textures and patterns in nature to inspire your art and walking observations:
-Patterns in Nature: Why the Natural World Looks the Way It Does by Philip Ball
-The Self-Made Tapestry by Phillip Ball
-Art Forms In Nature and other similar books by Ernst Haeckel on the wonder of nature's art forms.

⊙ Texture Rubbings: This is a fun activity of naturalists that you've probably tried in school. Bring along a lightweight piece of paper and a soft-lead pencil (between 2B-6B), or color pencils. Place your paper over interesting textures encountered on your walk and rub the pencils over it. Harder surfaces like rocks, stone walls or tree bark usually work better. Create a series of rubbings as studies in textural inspirations.

Buzzing with ideas or enjoyed a 'Textures' activity recently? Record them below:

Journal This:

What were your favorite textures in nature? What did you find utterly fascinating and creatively inspiring?

What do textures reveal about the journey or history of an object or natural element?

Did you encounter any patterns and textures that remind you of something else? Describe some of the more interesting associations.

Explorer's Notes

Related Cards:

How can you pair these related cards for a more interesting 'Textures' wonder-walk?
Color, Shape, Pareidolia, Study

Explorer's Notes

"Observe everything as if it is a marvelous, unknown phenomena - the blue sky, the crescent moon, the hoot of an owl on a midnight stroll."

Explorer's Notes

Naiveté

*Naiveté is beginner's mind. Walk as if five years old again -
untried, untrained, fresh to the magic of the world.
How will it inspire your art?*

One of my favorite games to play while on a wonder-walk is
to look at the world through fresh, unbiased eyes and wonder
about the things I take for granted around me. I imagine
myself living, 2000, 5000 years ago before the internet,
encyclopedias and scientific journals. How do I make sense
of sunrises and sunsets? What does it mean when the sky
turns black and tiny white blinking lights come out? Seeing
the world this way means falling in love with the ordinary
over and over again in a way that ignites my imagination and
inspire creative ideas.

Interpretations:
Innocence.
Beginner's mind.
Seeing through fresh eyes.
Candor, artlessness.
Child-like.

Realm Symbolism:
Magic-Making: The Creative Realm
Corresponding Symbolism: Fire, Passion, Intuition
Ask: How can you express the 'Naiveté' from your walk?

Observe This on Your Wonder-Walk:

Before your walk, wipe clean what you know about the world
around you. Observe everything as if it is a marvelous,
unknown phenomena - the blue sky, the crescent moon, the
hoot of an owl on a midnight stroll.

Notice how this changes the way you interact and feel about
the ordinary. As you walk, allow your inner child to wonder
and make up wild stories to explain what could be going on.

Walk as if you've never been to a place before. What would you
notice? What would you remember?

Activities to Try:

⊙ On one of your walks, imagine that you are an Early Human that lived 10,000 years ago and know nothing about the science behind celestial phenomena (the moon, the stars, the rising and setting sun). Write a short story about what it could be and what it might mean.

⊙ Ask Why. Pretend you're a child again, on a walk. Ask simple 'why' questions: Why is a tree leafy on top? Why are there waves on the shoreline? Make up the craziest, silliest answers you can think of. Let your imagination run wild! Draw, paint or sketch a surrealistic picture of this explanation.

⊙ On your next walk, draw or photograph the world around you in a way that obscures what they actually are. *For example, take a close-up shot of a field of flowers from an unusual angle so it looks mysterious. Photograph the striations of a rock in a way that makes it look like cake.* Print them out and write imaginative captions of what they could be (but aren't).

In a creative rut? These activities above will soon shake things up and re-ignite the fire!

Buzzing with ideas or enjoyed a 'Naiveté' activity recently? Record them below:

Journal This:

What did you notice when you wiped the proverbial slate clean? How did naiveté enrich the stories you told yourself about your surroundings?

Write down 2-3 of the more interesting explanations and stories you came up with on your walk. Can you turn this into an art project? A painting, a poem, an anthology of stories?

> **Explorer's Notes**

Related Cards:

How can you pair these related cards for a more interesting 'Naiveté' wonder-walk?

Disruption, Play, Wonder, Pretend

> **Explorer's Notes**

"It's that deliberate surrender to the moment, the glee of going down hidden alleys, unmarked roads, abandoned estates."

Explorer's Notes

Play

Skip, hop, play. Climb trees or step in puddles.
Be light-hearted in your walk and art today.

A playful walk to me is kicking off my shoes and skipping over tidepools. Leaving my maps at home and getting lost on a new hike or neighborhood. It's that deliberate surrender to the moment, the glee of going down hidden alleys, unmarked roads, abandoned estates. To play on a walk is to climb trees, press up against store windows, peek through intriguing openings. Always a spontaneous adventure and a light-hearted exploration, its effervescence relaxes me and never fails to bubble over to inspire my creativity pursuits.

Interpretations:
Fun, joyousness, gaiety.
Curiosity, exploration, experiments.
Spontaneity, getting lost, surrendering.
Uninhibited, untethered.
Mischief, tricksy.

Realm Symbolism:
Magic-Making: The Creative Realm
Corresponding Symbolism: Fire, Passion, Intuition
Ask: How can you express the sense of 'Play' from your walk?

Observe This on Your Wonder-Walk:

What are some ways to play on your walk? Can you climb any trees? Squeeze through rock openings, wade in a river?

Instead of following your usual route or directions, let your curiosity lead the way. Take the path that meanders through the wooded area. Follow the heron flying by. Observe if spontaneity makes your walk more or less fun.

What happens if you alter the way your body moves? Walk backwards, on your hands, leap from rock to rock, step between the cracks. Observe how this changes the mood of the walk and what you notice differently around you.

Activities to Try:

⊙ Tree Play: Climb the most interesting tree you can find where you live. Once on top, take a series of photos from that vantage point (be safe!). Savor the creative possibilities of a perspective not possible at ground level.

⊙ Ideation Adventure: Plan a day's adventure to a town nearby with your Creative Explorer Kit (see Part I for how to assemble one). Make no plans for what to do or see that day. Leave your Google Maps at home. Wander instead, be spontaneous, go where your heart, joy and curiosity leads you. Jot down any creative ideas that pop up as you relax into your playful wonder-walks. (This works particularly well when you are marinating on a project.) Stop frequently to sketch or journal your surroundings.

⊙ A Picnic Adventure: Pack an elaborate picnic like the ones in your favorite adventure books as a child. Have fun creating a wonderful spread to enjoy outdoors. Try new recipes. Make them bento-beautiful. Strap your lunch to your bicycle or backpack and head out for a day in nature or town. As you walk, look out for the perfect place to picnic. Unroll your blanket, set up and enjoy your spread with a glad heart. Celebrate with a cartwheel or two.

Buzzing with ideas or enjoyed a 'Play' activity recently? Record them below:

Journal This:

What were the most enjoyable parts of your playful walk? Why?

Did changing how your body moves made a walk more fun? What would you incorporate into your other walks?

What did you learn about being playful today? Did any creative ideas come up?

Explorer's Notes

Related Cards:

How can you pair these related cards for a more interesting 'Play' wonder-walk?

Follow the Rabbit, Mood Painting, Enchantment, Disruption

Explorer's Notes

"**S**tep into
enchanting,
miniature worlds
more marvelous
than our own."

Explorer's Notes

Thumbelina

How would the world look like if you were as small as Thumbelina? Express this creatively.

The story of Thumbelina, a tiny girl born inside a flower, who slept in a walnut shell and sailed the world on a leaf, was my first introduction to the wonders of altering scale and perspective. In this fairy tale, her adventures as a diminutive person in an ordinary world are both magical and frightening, kindling my imagination like no other. This card invites us to look closer at the littlest details around us for creative inspiration, to let ourselves step into enchanting, miniature worlds more marvelous than our own.

Interpretations:
Seeing the world through Thumbelina's eyes
Looking closer at details normally missed
Imagining ourselves in miniature, tiny worlds
Open-mindedness to changing perspective

Realm Symbolism:
Magic-Making: The Creative Realm
Corresponding Symbolism: Fire, Passion, Intuition
Ask: How can you creatively express a 'Thumbelina' walk?

Observe This on Your Wonder-Walk:

Walk as if you were as small as Thumbelina, where rain droplets could sweep you away and a harmless squirrel looms terrifyingly large. Crouch down and peek at the worlds hiding by your feet - under the grass and on forest floors, in the crevices of rocks and fallen tree trunks. Peer into hearts of flowers, in between plant and tree foliage and moss-covered rocks.

Bring along a magnifying glass or a miniature toy animal and keep your eyes open for fascinating miniature worlds so unlike our own. Imagine leaves as entire trees, flowers as big as houses, reeds like skyscrapers. How would a butterfly or ladybird appear to Thumbelina? What about the friendly neighborhood cat? What can you imagine seeing if you were small enough to climb a vine plant or ride on a snail's shell?

Activities to Try:

⊙ A Thumbelina Creative Adventure: Plan a day trip to places that would delight your inner 'Thumbelina'. Ideas: *Botanical gardens, tide pools, forests, wildflower trails, rocky landscapes, etc.*
-Bring along a miniature toy animal or doll as your Thumbelina, and to provide a sense of scale.
-Pack your camera, sketchbook and/or paints.
-As you walk, look out for interesting miniature worlds to insert your little toy animal or doll.
-Take a series of photos, sketch or paint these magical scenes starring your Thumbelina toy.
-Have fun; allow your imagination to run wild!

⊙ Miniature World Inspirations: Visit a library or a bookstore and look for children's books or fairy tales featuring 'Thumbelina' perspectives. From illustrated books like the delightful *Brambly Hedge series by Jill Barklem, and* <u>Adventures of Pip</u> *by Enid Blyton, to a classic fairy tale like* "The Elves and The Shoemaker", the children's section is filled with imaginative and wonderfully vivid tales of little beings in big worlds.
-Select a few to read or re-read.
-Alternatively, watch *Nature's Miniature Miracles*, a fantastically filmed documentary series on survival as nature's small guys.
-Plan a Thumbelina Creative Adventure inspired by the book or documentary.

Buzzing with ideas or enjoyed a 'Thumbelina' activity recently? Record them below:

Journal This:

Where would you like to explore if you were as small as Thumbelina? What (miniature) worlds would be fascinting to you? What would be scary?

What other books or movies told from altered perspectives did you love? Describe what you loved about them.

Describe a place you've been recently or in the past that would make a great Thumbelina adventure. Why?

Explorer's Notes

Related Cards:

How can you pair these related cards for a more interesting 'Thumbelina' wonder-walk?

Hidden, Fairy Worlds, Wonder, Pretend

Explorer's Notes

"What messages might nature be sending to you?"

Explorer's Notes

Symbolism

A deeper meaning hides in the ordinary. Notice and express your recurring symbols from your walks in a medium of choice.

The world is richer and more alive when we see hidden meanings all around us, experiencing nature as if we are one with it, instead of an entity separate from it - our inner and outer realms interweaving seamlessly. A flowing river, a bridge, a feather on the ground, all vibrate with meaning and story when we dissolve the boundaries between ourselves and the physical world. What am I meant to pay attention to today? What would this represent in my journey?

Interpretations:
A deeper meaning or signification
Metaphor or allegory
Allusion
An object representing another
Suggesting mystical ideas, emotions or states of mind

Realm Symbolism:
Magic-Making: The Creative Realm
Corresponding Symbolism: Fire, Passion, Intuition
Ask: How can you express the 'Symbolism' from your walk?

Observe This on Your Wonder-Walk:

What we notice around us hides myriad clues about our feelings and thoughts at the moment. Do you envy the ease and constancy of the flowing river? Are you looking for a bridge to the other side of a niggling problem? What is the mighty Blue Heron, still and attentive on the riverbank, really saying to you?

You might take the same walk everyday but notice different things. Observe if anything is out of the ordinary. What is particularly riveting, fascinating or compelling today?

What messages might nature be sending to you?

Activities to Try:

⊙ A Symbolism Diary: Start one of your own. Record the animals, plants, objects and events that capture your attention from your day's wonder-walk. Begin an entry by recording your encounter. Describe what happened, what you were feeling or thinking at the time and what it could possible signify.

Sketch, paint or attach a photograph of the symbol in the entry. Include notes of researched natural history, habitat or traits. Additionally, look up its cultural, archetypal and historic meanings.

This activity would enrich your dossier of personal symbols and help you build a bridge between your inner and outer worlds.

⊙ Nature Altar: Curate a nature altar or curio cabinet and fill it with meaningful treasures from wonder-walks and travels that were particularly symbolic. Gather only totems and symbols that align with your current life journey or project.

⊙ Totem Cards: Create a set of totem cards from the recurring symbols on your wonder-walks. You can collage them from National Geographic magazines or draw and paint them from reference photos. Write a short paragraph on the back of the card about the encounter and what the symbol means to you.

Buzzing with ideas or enjoyed a 'Symbolism' activity recently? Record them below:

Journal This:

What animals, plants, objects or events from your wonder-walk evoked a strong emotion today? Describe the symbols' natural traits or characteristics.

What do you think it could mean to your personal journey right now? What does it symbolize?

How will your symbolic encounter affect your actions today? Describe what you'll change or do.

Explorer's Notes

Related Cards:

How can you pair these related cards for a more interesting 'Symbolism' wonder-walk?

Notice, Intuition, Flora, Fauna

Explorer's Notes

"What are the signs that wildlife is about, even if you can't see them?"

Explorer's Notes

Fauna

Observe or embody nature's creatures.
Let your favorite fauna sightings today inspire a project.

An encounter with the elusive bear, owl or wild boar is always a special moment. Mountain lion tracks in the mud, coyote howls at twilight, spider webs glistening with dewdrops. Seen or unseen, fauna is all around us, an integral part of the intricate tapestry of life. Know the creatures, big or small, that live and roam the land alongside you. Notice their tracks, learn their traits, understand their habits. Are they endangered? Are they migratory? Where do they feed and nest?
Let them inform and inspire you.

Interpretations:
Local or regional wildlife
The Animal Kingdom
Spirit or totem animals
Symbols or archetypes

Realm Symbolism:
Magic-Making: The Creative Realm
Corresponding Symbolism: Fire, Passion, Intuition
Ask: How can you express the 'Fauna' from your walk?

Observe This on Your Wonder-Walk:

Look out for tracks or scat on your walk. What are the signs that wildlife is about, even if you can't see them? Leave the headphones at home, especially at dawn or dusk, when the dim light brings much wildlife out to hunt.

Listen out for their birdsong, the pitter-patter of paws and claws, the gentle rustling of antler against branch. Watch out for the swirling of sea birds over bait ball or the blow of a humpback whale far out in the ocean. Can you tell a soaring bird by its wing shape? Is it a hawk or a vulture? Falcon or kite?

Notice what times of the day you're most likely to encounter wildlife. Note any distinguishing features, colors, and shape so you can look them up later.

Activities to Try:

⊙ The Naturalist Sketchbook: Start one to record your wildlife encounters. Feel free to combine this with your Symbolism Diary (from the Symbolism activity page). A blank journal with no lines is best so you are free to sketch and diagram. Choose a paper that is thick enough to hold up to light washes of watercolor as well as pen and ink.

(Nice-to-have: Download the iNaturalist app on your phone to help you identify the animals you encounter.)

⊙ Natural History Adventure: Visit a local natural history museum with your Naturalist Sketchbook to study, sketch or photograph local wildlife that would be otherwise difficult to spot in nature. Pay attention to their skeletal structure, their habitat and feeding habits, the color, texture and shape of their skin, fur or feathers.

⊙ Wildlife Poem: Write a poem or haiku about one of your favorite wildlife encounters. Be as lyrical and metaphorical as you want. Incorporate what you noticed most, what enchanted you, how the magical event happened.

Buzzing with ideas or enjoyed a 'Fauna' activity recently? Record them below:

Journal This:

What animals are you most drawn to in the wild? Why?

What animals would like to find out more about? List some fun ways you can study this animal in more detail.

Describe your most exciting and intriguing wildlife encounter. What was going on at the time? Where were you? Why was it a significant event?

Explorer's Notes

Related Cards:

How can you pair these related cards for a more interesting 'Fauna' wonder-walk?

Pretend, Symbolism, Shape, Poetry

Explorer's Notes

> "It invites us to abstract our responses to place, character and atmosphere into visceral expressions of the heart."

Explorer's Notes

Mood Painting

How do you feel on your walk today?
Intuitively paint your mood with value, color and texture.

Mood painting is pouring our souls on paper, intuitively capturing our fleeting emotions and impressions of an exterior world. How does a sunrise make us feel? What emotions emerge on a dark moonlit night? How can we express the serenity of a glassy, placid lake? This card invites us to abstract our responses to place, character and atmosphere into visceral expressions of the heart - pictures, paintings, poetry; and to celebrate the intersection between nature, emotion, and creative play.

Interpretations:
Visceral or emotional expressions
Abstract paintings or writings of nature
A deep, lyrical and poetic understanding or empathy
Capturing an atmosphere creatively

Realm Symbolism:
Magic-Making: The Creative Realm
Corresponding Symbolism: Fire, Passion, Intuition
Ask: What 'Mood Paintings' will your walk inspire?

Observe This on Your Wonder-Walk:

What is the current mood or atmosphere of your surroundings? Is it cheerfully sunny and warm? Calmingly peaceful and tranquil? How are you responding emotionally to the world around you?

Observe the colors and textures you're noticing, and what they're evoking in you - *e.g.* the rose gold of sunset over a still, marshy bay makes me feel pleasantly squishy inside. Observe how your emotions and physical senses are interacting with each other as you walk.

Notice the subtle nuances in color, texture and shape all around you and if they feel soothing or dramatic, harmonious or lively, pleasing or disturbing.

Activities to Try:

⊙ A Mood Painting Adventure: Practice mood-painting your wonder-walk experiences.
-Grab your Creative Adventure Kit (see Part I) or assemble one and head out for a walk. Mood paint the first thing that catches your eye or your heart.
-Instead of trying to capture the scene representationally (literally) using your paints, express how you feel instead. Choose colors that intuitively correspond with your emotions: *e.g. yellow for joy, pink for passion, gray for peace, etc.* With practice, eventually you'll develop your own symbolic color language.

⊙ Creative Challenge: Try mood painting with a camera, with different types of art media (pencils, pastels, collage, embroidery, etc.) or with writing. Would you capture dreamy, abstract photos that are emotionally evocative rather than literal? How would you write the feelings of a place? Would it be poetry or prose?

⊙ Journey Mood Painting: Using a wide piece of medium-weight watercolor or printmaking paper, create your mood painting as a journey with a beginning, middle and an end.
-Journal your feelings and observations before, during and after your walk. Choose a color and texture to represent each stage. Work loosely.
-Using your paints, translate each stage of the walk into an abstracted mood painting. Have fun!

Buzzing with ideas or enjoyed a 'Mood Painting' activity recently? Record them below:

Journal This:

What feelings came up before, during and after your walk?

What do you think is the overall mood or message around your walk? Did it change throughout or stay the same?

Describe how you felt on your walk today in the language of color, texture and shape.

How did it feel to translate your walking experience into a mood painting?

Explorer's Notes

Related Cards:

How can you pair these related cards for a more interesting 'Mood-Painting' wonder-walk?

Synesthesia, Color, First Love, Spirit of Place

Explorer's Notes

"The world around me becomes an ever-open box of paints ready to dip in anytime."

Explorer's Notes

Color

Colors reveal mood, emotions, stories.
How can you express this part of your walk creatively?

Color is a feeling, a soul expression, a tale of many hues.
When I am on a wonder-walk, my eyes take in the colors of my
surroundings, and often a color story begins to emerge. The
rich mauves of dried eucalyptus leaves, the deep indigo of the
night sky, the silvery blue-grays of tree trunks in dimming
light. Some days all I see is the pale green of lace lichen and
other days the blush pink of California buckwheat catches
my heart. My feelings and thoughts color what I see and vice
versa. The world around me becomes an ever-open box of
paints ready to dip in anytime.

Interpretations:
Hue, shade, tone, tint
A shade of meaning
A feeling or mood
Pigment or dye

Realm Symbolism:
Magic-Making: The Creative Realm
Corresponding Symbolism: Fire, Passion, Intuition
Ask: How can you express the 'Colors' from your walk?

Observe This on Your Wonder-Walk:

Notice the colors you're drawn to today in your surroundings.
Observe when a pattern begins to emerge. Are you attracted
to the same hues, shades, tints, and tones over and over again
as you walk? Notice how colors look side by side, how they
complement or contrast each other.

The silvery brown of cypress trees against the gold of dried
grass. Pale moon against navy sky.

Observe and document how the colors you're seeing around
you make you feel. Peaceful or excited? Dynamic or serene?
Are there pops of color dotting the landscape?
Where are they from?

Activities to Try:

⊙ The Color Walk: Take a walk during your favorite time of the day to observe colors in nature. Alternatively, visit a plant conservatory, nursery or botanical garden - anywhere where there are abundant colors to electrify the senses. Experiment with creative color similes or poems to describe what you're experiencing: *sky as pink as cotton candy, pond as green as emeralds, rose petals the color of rich cream.*

⊙ Color Story Play: Create a Color Story from your wonder-walk today with 3-5 colors you were drawn to the most during the walk. You may photograph or gather treasures from nature (be sure to check if you're allowed to) to inspire the color-mixing back in your studio. Alternatively, bring a Creative Adventure Kit (see Part I on how to assemble one) and mix the colors onsite in your sketchbook.

⊙ Use this Color Story to inspire a painting or art journal page. Have fun: explore different ways to combine the colors in the Color Story. Try a page with just 1 color, then a page with 2 colors, 3 colors, etc.

Buzzing with ideas or enjoyed a 'Color' activity recently? Record them below:

Journal This:

What colors caught your heart and eye today? Describe how these colors made you feel.

Why do you think you noticed certain colors more than others today? Does it reflect what you are pondering or going through in your life right now?

When are your favorite times of the day (or year) for observing colors outdoors? Is it dawn or dusk, fall or spring? Why?

Explorer's Notes

Related Cards:

How can you pair these related cards for a more interesting 'Color' wonder-walk?

Flora, Dusk, Mood Painting, Fauna

Explorer's Notes

"It's the magical, liminal hour when the hidden underworld stirs, just before darkness descends all around us."

Dusk

Dusk is a sunset, a twilight, a threshold to darkness.
Creativity comes alive in its magical light, what else?

Enchanted is the world stained a soft, rosy glow, in that hour just before all turns the moody blue of twilight. The owls are out, silent and watching, rabbits dart about bravely, the occasional deer venture shyly out into the open wild. Dusk is the magical, liminal hour when the hidden underworld stirs, just before darkness descends all around us. It is one of my favorite times for wonder-walking - a dimming world comes alive in magical ways that ignite my creativity and imagination like no other hour before or after it.

Interpretations:
Crepescule, twilight, blue hour
Sunset, sundown, golden hour
Liminal time between day and night (light and dark)
Darkness is descending, changing light

Realm Symbolism:
Magic-Making: The Creative Realm
Corresponding Symbolism: Fire, Passion, Intuition
Ask: How does a 'Dusk' walk inspire you?

Observe This on Your Wonder-Walk:

Be vigilant in the hour just before and after the sun disappears over the horizon. Notice when the sky changes colors from golden to violet to dazzling shades of crimson and pink. Take note of how long each transition takes.

Observe how the gradual easing into nocturne transforms the world around you. Do ordinary scenes transform into magical, mysterious places as the light changes from rosy hues to eerie blues? What do you notice that you didn't in the bright of day?

Be on the lookout for wildlife emerging to hunt. Can you recognize them by sound even if you can't see them in the dimming light? Listen out for gentle rustling, distinct calls and the pitter-patter of a hidden presence all around you.

125

Activities to Try:

⊙ Day and Dusk: Take a photograph, or paint the same location (*e.g. a favorite place, tree, path*) at two different times of the day: outdoors at midday; and during the rosy, golden or blue hour of dusk. Place the two pictures side by side and compare them: How are they different? Is it the colors? The mood? The emotions they evoke? The differing creatures presented? Journal your thoughts and findings.

⊙ A Dusk Mood Painting: Refer to the chapter on 'Mood Painting' and make one at your favorite wonder-walk location outdoors at dusk. Use the colors of sunset, dimming light, shadow, or the atmosphere of twilight to inspire you.

⊙ A Story of Dusk: Take a wonder-walk at your favorite location where you can walk through the changing light right into the darkness of night. Write a short story or a poem about what you imagine happens at dusk based on what you experienced. Be as imaginative and creative as you can. It can be realistic (true to life) or fantastical, and any style in between.

Buzzing with ideas or enjoyed a 'Dusk' activity recently? Record them below:

Journal This:

Describe how your favorite places for walks transform during dusk. What are the physical changes? Is it quieter or louder, more or less serene? How does the changing light affect it?

Does it *feel* different to walk these places at dusk? Why?

What was the most creatively inspiring aspect of your dusk wonder-walk?

Explorer's Notes

Related Cards:

How can you pair these related cards for a more interesting 'Dusk' wonder-walk?

Color, Dawn, Darkness, Fauna

Explorer's Notes

"What hidden
or interesting
shapes do you
see if you look
closer around
you?"

Explorer's Notes

Shape

Sketch the land like an artist.
Find the shapes, the contours, the striations.

Shapes define so much of the world around us that it is
inevitable we would connect to some of them more than others.
There are shapes that convey a deep sense of journey - the path,
the labyrinth, the crossroads, and ones whose very simplicity
belie complex symbolic narratives - the crescent, the circle, the
star. This card invites us to study and express the shapes that
delight us in nature and our surroundings, and through it,
a reverence and celebration of the creative magic in the
everyday ordinary.

Interpretations:
Outline, contour, silhouette
A specific form or figure
Patterns, organizations
A physical construct

Realm Symbolism:
Magic-Making: The Creative Realm
Corresponding Symbolism: Fire, Passion, Intuition
Ask: How can you express the 'Shapes' from your walk?

Observe This on Your Wonder-Walk:

Have you noticed on your walks that shape is often easier to
spot than color? For example, we usually spy a path through
the forest faster than we would notice the gradiating colors
of the foliage around it. As you walk, observe how the shape
of something makes it more or less prominent to you, or other
forms of life around it.

What hidden or interesting shapes do you see if you look closer
around you? Observe the shape of plants and their leaves,
flowers and seeds. Notice if it's spiraled, fan-shaped, triangular.
Pay attention to the shapes of insects and wildlife and how this
allows them to blend in when it matters. Observe if there's a
difference in shapes of living versus non-living elements.
Pay attention to the big and the small, the many, the clustered
and the singular.

Activities to Try:

⊙ Capturing Shapes: Explore observing and then capturing shapes in nature using your choice of visual media - *e.g. photography, pencils, watercolors, acrylics, oils, etc.*
-Assemble a Creative Adventure Kit (see Part I) with your favorite media for this activity. Include a sketchbook or a clipboard of papers.
-Head out for your walk and look out for shapes in your surroundings - big (*e.g. buildings, trees, hills*) or small (*e.g. leaves, flowers, shells.*)
-See if you can spot these common natural shapes: *fans, circles/spheres, spirals, branches, stars, triangles.* What others did you notice?
-Photograph, sketch or paint your favorites. It can be abstract or representational, as long as it's fun for you!

⊙ Shapes and Mood Painting: Refer to the 'Mood Painting' chapter and work from a completed mood painting. Add to this the shapes you noticed on your walk using complementary colored pencils, pens, embroidery or paint. You can even try collaging with photos and magazine cut-outs. Challenge: See how these shape mood paintings can be detailed to create a scene or story - *a fantasy underwater world, an enchanted forest, an abstraction of emotions...*have fun, be playful!

Buzzing with ideas or enjoyed a 'Shape' activity recently? Record them below:

Journal This:

What shapes are you drawn to over and over on your walks?

What are your favorite shapes in nature? What never fails to fascinate you when you see them? Why?

What kind of shapes do you find yourself inspired to express creatively? How would you express them; what do they symbolize for you?

Explorer's Notes

Related Cards:

How can you pair these related cards for a more interesting 'Shape' wonder-walk?

Texture, Color, Notice, Hidden

Explorer's Notes

"I let myelf imagine a world where things aren't what they appear to be, that strange events can and do happen."

Explorer's Notes

Dream

Chase the walk that makes you dream of other worlds.
Free-associate this in your medium of choice.

Some days, when there is just the right amount of fog in the
air, when the eerie blue of twilight cloaks the land, or when
the full moon looms like a large lantern over the hill, I have
this strange feeling that I've wandered into a dream. On these
days I let myelf imagine a world where things aren't what they
appear to be, that strange events can and do happen.
My senses are heightened, my imagination piqued and
everything seems new and unreal. A dream wonder-walk is a
deliberate suspension of disbelief, a choice to see the world as
if at any moment, reality can shift and bend.

Interpretations:
Surrealism
An imaginary world
Between waking and sleeping
The liminal or in-between land
A flight of fancy

Realm Symbolism:
Magic-Making: The Creative Realm
Corresponding Symbolism: Fire, Passion, Intuition
Ask: How would you express a 'Dream' walk?

Observe This on Your Wonder-Walk:

As you walk, allow your imagination to wander in unexpected
and playful ways. Look at the twisted, gnarly branches of oak
trees as if they were arms of an ancient sea monster turned
into stone by a curse. Perhaps that small island in the ocean
was once a powerful ancient kingdom.

Conjure fantastical stories to describe what happens to the
landscape at certain special times - the full moon, at dawn or
dusk - would the cluster of rocks turn into waking giants?

Seek out the quirky and strange in the world around you.
Notice if anything is out of the ordinary.

Activities to Try:

⊙ Surrealism Study: Study some famous surrealist paintings - in person, if possible; in books or on Pinterest if you can't make it to an exhibit. Take a look at René Magritte or Salvadore Dali's works. Then create your own dossier of favorite dreamscape paintings and artists as inspiration.

⊙ Land Art Adventure: Visit and experience amazing Land Art sites in person (look up a list of this online). These are life-sized sculptures or installations created from organic materials and installed out in nature, often in wondrous, mind-bending ways - *portals in trees, giant nests, hanging cocoons.* Journal, paint or photograph the experience.

⊙ Dreamscapes: Visit an otherworldly natural site near you. *Great examples are Mono Lake (tufa towers) or Devil's Postpile (basalt columns) in California.* Create a series of photographs, paintings or stories depicting the dream-like atmosphere of the site.

⊙ The Dream Walk: Take a walk during the most magical, dream-like time of the day or season - during foggy days, blue hour at dusk (transitioning to night), or early morning (transitioning to day). Write a short poem about the experience.

Buzzing with ideas or enjoyed a 'Dream' activity recently? Record them below:

Journal This:

Describe in detail the most dream-like walk you've ever had.
What made it seem almost unreal? What was unusual about it?

What are some of your favorite stories, movies or books
involving dreams and dreamscapes?

What are some otherworldly, dream-like places you'd like to
visit? Make a list and pick your first one to plan a trip to.

What makes a place or walk strange and dream-like to you?

Explorer's Notes

Related Cards:

How can you pair these related cards for a more
interesting 'Dream' wonder-walk?

Naiveté, Fairy Worlds, Pareidolia, Thumbelina

Explorer's Notes

What evokes strong emotions?

Truth-Finding
The Inner Realm

"A place can ache.
A place can haunt.
A place can shimmer
with laughters past.

Spirit of Place

A physical inhabitation, a belonging, a memory.
What is the spirit of this place, what does it mean to you?

In any place we tread, there is an aliveness, a soul, a sense of what the land is about. There are stories in every rock, tree and flower. Tales to tell within brick walls and peeling paint. When we honor the spirit of a place, we honor what it was, what it is and what it can be. When I walk a place I entwine my own stories with that of the land, and those of others before me. A place can ache. A place can haunt. A place can shimmer with laughters past. I feel it and it feels me. A house, a wood, a city street echo with many invisible voices yearning to be heard.

Interpretations:
Genius loci.
Story of a place.
Essence or character.
Land soul or psyche.
An invisible presence or aliveness.

Realm Symbolism:
Truth-Finding: The Inner Realm
Corresponding Symbolism: Water, Emotion, Feeling
Ask: What feelings would a 'Spirit of Place' walk evoke?

Observe This on Your Wonder-Walk:

As you walk, observe what defines the place. Are there particular flora and fauna varieties that give the place a distinct character? How long have the buildings been around? Who built it? Why? Ponder what this place might have meant to its early occupants. What dreams did they have for it?

How does walking this place make you feel? Is there an invisible presence or aliveness in the air? Does it feel like a happy or melancholic place? Old or new?

Notice the feelings that come up even if you don't understand them. Your intuition may be picking up subtle cues from your environment that lightly pierces your consciousness.

Activities to Try:

The Spirit of Place Walk: Plan a visit to a historically meaningful site. Preferably one you've never been to before or know little about. Bring a journal and go for a walk, stopping occasionally to immerse and ponder.

Open your heart and senses. Let yourself *feel* the place. Get to know it as you would someone you've just met. Ask it questions:

Hello, why are you here?
What's your journey like so far?
Tell me a funny/sad story?
How do you feel right now?

You may find yourself swept away by the beautiful remnants of a rich and vibrant past or sad and indignant over the injustice in a war-torn community. Observe details, let feelings wash over you as you explore the site. Record your thoughts. Sketch them out. Photograph the corners that evoke the strongest emotions.

After your walk, if possible, find out the actual history of the place. What feelings corresponded with real events that took place? Do you feel like you've gotten to know its spirit?

Buzzing with ideas or enjoyed a 'Spirit of Place' activity recently? Record them below:

Journal This:

Describe in detail how a place made you feel as you walked through it.

Without researching first, describe what you think is the story of a place you've recently visited and walked? Does this place remind you of any other places you've been to, real or fictional?

What were you drawn to on your walk in this place? Would finding more about it change how you feel about it?

Explorer's Notes

Related Cards:

How can you pair these related cards for a more interesting 'Spirit of Place' wonder-walk?

Story, Listen, Connect, Immersion

Explorer's Notes

"**W**hen the physical world meets or exceeds the magic of our imagination..."

Explorer's Notes

Enchantment

Slow down and reflect on all that enchants you in your outer world. What does it reveal about your spirit and soul?

Enchantment is our heart aching with an emotion beyond experiencing beauty. It's the expansiveness that sometimes makes us cry, but mostly reminds us how grateful we are to be alive this instance. Enchantment is when the physical world meets or exceeds the magic of our imagination. It is everything sublime, transcendental, otherwordly, but also meaningful and soul-filled. This card invites us to explore all the ways life enchants us, the truths it reveals about ourselves, and how we might be transformed by it.

Interpretations:
Enthrallment, mesmerized, spellbound
A sublime, transcendental experience
Aesthetic arrest; beyond beauty
A sublime, amplified existence

Realm Symbolism:
Truth-Finding: The Inner Realm
Corresponding Symbolism: Water, Emotion, Feeling
Ask: What inner truths might an 'Enchantment' walk reveal?

Observe This on Your Wonder-Walk:

Notice what takes your breath away and makes you a little emotional. That secret meadow of flowers so magical it brings tears to your eyes. The majestic rainforest walk you've been dreaming about since you were a little girl.

Observe if any sights on your walk becomes so captivating that you lose track of time. An ethereal sunset on a cloudy day after a rainfall - all double rainbows, moody violet skies and gold-rimmed clouds. What held you under its spell?

Remember the experiences that amplify your aliveness and enthrall your senses completely. A magical light show in a botanical garden at night, a serene walk on a white snowy day.

Activities to Try:

⊙ Exploring Enchantment: What happens if you are regularly enchanted in your life? Using an Explorer Chart (see Part III), map out meaningful experiences that take your breath away and move you deeply. *E.g. visits to the symphony, sunset walks with a loved one, a ballet show every season, a candlelit event at a local botanic garden, a rose garden tea party.*
   - Choose an experience to enjoy every week. Journal how you felt after, if it enchanted you, and if you learned anything about yourself.

⊙ Re-Enchant Your Home: What simple activities or objects infuse meaning, magic and soul in your home life? Make a list of these little enchantments and introduce them into your life gradually, e.g. *A beautiful morning ritual with aromatherapy candles and a hand-bound journal; a large bouquet of fresh flowers on your dining table every week; magical paintings on your living room wall; creatively plated meals, etc.* Journal your feelings and discoveries after implementing them for a month.

⊙ An Enchanted Walk: Select one of the cards in the deck for this activity. I love *Dawn, Dusk, Flora, The Woods,* and *Fairy Worlds.* Head out for a walk, refer to the previous page on what to observe while out. Journal your feelings and epiphanies on enchantment afterward.

Buzzing with ideas or enjoyed a 'Enchantment' activity recently? Record them below:

Journal This:

What does enchantment mean to you?

Describe a time when a physical experience was so sublime that it exceeded your imagination of it. Why do you think you were so captivated by it?

What are some ways you can re=enchant your everyday?

Explorer's Notes

Related Cards:

How can you pair these related cards for a more interesting 'Enchantment' wonder-walk?

Dream, Fairy Worlds, Wonder, The Woods

Explorer's Notes

"The woods speak of mysterious depths within and without, of places we have yet to explore, may not explore."

Explorer's Notes

The Woods

*Enigmatic, mysterious and full of life, the woods is for
exploring the unknown within and without.*

Whenever I enter the woods, be it a live oak grove, an ancient
redwood forest or the misty jungles of Borneo, the hush of
reverence washes over me. The wisdom and vibrancy of the
trees and all that make the woods its home is palpable even
if invisible. The woods serve as a reminder that much of life
is a mystery and many of nature's wonders are hidden in dark
crevices and ominous shadows. That there are unseen eyes
everywhere, watching, knowing, waiting. The woods speak of
mysterious depths within and without, of places we have yet
to explore, may not explore. They ask: what do we really know
about ourselves and the world? Are we brave enough to enter
that which we don't completely understand?

Interpretations:
A dark and mysterious place.
An enchanted forest.
Entering the unknown.
Facing our fears.

Realm Symbolism:
Truth-Finding: The Inner Realm
Corresponding Symbolism: Water, Emotion, Feeling
Ask: What inner truths might a walk in 'The Woods' reveal?

Observe This on Your Wonder-Walk:

All woods have their own spirit of place. Moss, lichen or
redwood sorrel can transform ordinary forests into serene,
ethereal fairy worlds. Likewise, large tropical leaves can make
you feel as you've wandered back into primitive times.

Observe what makes your neck of the woods distinct and how
you feel as you walk in it. What evokes strong emotions?

Notice the tree trunks, if they're twisted or gnarly or full of
mysterious witchy eyes like those on aspen trees. Observe if
the shape of the tree canopy feels cocooning or awe-inspiring.

Activities to Try:

- ⊙ *Shinrin-Yoku* (Forest Bathing): *Shinrin-Yoku* is the Japanese practice of forest bathing. To explore this therapeutic activity, look for a forest (or a park with trees) near you. Consider the trails, slopes, noise level, plants, luminescence and types of trees that please you the most. Find a spot in the forest that's comfortable and begin a leisurely forest-walk, letting all of your senses soak in the surroundings. Release your troubles and slow down by paying attention to the sights, smells, and sounds of the forest.
  Try these while forest-bathing: picnicking, plant observation, meditation, T'ai chi or yoga.

- ⊙ Forest Rhythms: Get to know your favorite forest through every season - all four if you live where it's a possibility (night versus day if you don't). Journal in the same spot each time. Get to know its rhythm and occupants. Observe and record how it makes you feel when the flowers are blooming, when the leaves turn color, or when it's barren and snow-covered. Create a series of paintings or photographs to express how the forest changes cyclically and how it affects you.

- ⊙ Quest in the Woods: Name your favorite woods where you live something fanciful, like you would have as a child. *The Forest of Golden Light. The Shadowy Woods.* Before your next walk, think of a problem you'd like to untangle. Imagine yourself as a fairy tale character on a quest through this magical forest which will reveal answers, hidden in plain sight. Every bent branch, overturned stone or wildlife encounter could be a clue.

Buzzing with ideas or enjoyed an activity in 'The Woods' recently? Record them below:

Journal This:

What were some of your favorite stories from childhood involving the woods? Why were you drawn to these stories?

Describe your most memorable woodland experience. Why?

What feelings came up when you walked the woods? Journal both the light and dark emotions. What might you have encountered in the woods that sparked these feelings?

Explorer's Notes

Related Cards:

How can you pair these related cards for a more interesting wonder-walk in 'The Woods'?

Spirit of Place, Darkness, Hidden, Fairy Worlds

Explorer's Notes

"Stroll the paths that feel like a big warm hug."

Explorer's Notes

Intuition

Walk with intuition as your only guide.
Where would it lead you, what would it reveal?

An intuitive walk is spontaneous, surprising, unexpected.
We follow a smooth trail of white pebbles lit by soul light, guided
by curiosity, wonder, emotion. We cast aside all maps and plans
and go where the inner winds blow. Where can I go that nourishes
my spirit at this moment? What places can I explore that will
light my heart today? It's a walk that encourages us to ponder
the hidden messages in the rabbits we chase, the doorways - real
or imagined - that we enter, every flower or plant we can't help
touching. We allow ourselves to be tugged along an invisible
string that threads through our physical places but leads us into
the unexplored depths of inner ones.

Interpretations:
Instinct or hunch
The unconscious mind
A premonition or foreknowledge
An inner guidance or knowing

Realm Symbolism:
Truth-Finding: The Inner Realm
Corresponding Symbolism: Water, Emotion, Feeling
Ask: What inner truths might an 'Intuition' walk reveal?

Observe This on Your Wonder-Walk:

Release all expectations for your intuitive walk. The objective
is to take the walk that your soul needs most at this moment. As
you walk, pay attention to what around you lights you up and
makes you smile. Stroll the paths that feel like a big warm hug.
Ask yourself: *What would I most like to see right now? Do I crave
watching waves crashing against the rocky cliffs? Where can I
explore that would fill my heart today? Is it the Natural History
Museum? The Conservatory at the Botanical Gardens? The vintage
shops on Main Street?*

Much like the 'Listen' or 'Notice' walks, pay attention to what you
notice in your physical world around you that moves you. This
can reveal thoughts and feelings you might not be aware of.

Activities to Try:

⊙ Beautiful Inquiry Walk: Before you set out on a walk, think of a problem you've been stuck on. Frame it into a question (Beautiful Inquiry). Head out for a walk somewhere that brings you joy and fills your heart. Bring your journal or notebook with you. Follow what you notice as you tuck your Beautiful Inquiry away. As you enjoy yourself and sink into your walk, surroundings and activities, your unconscious mind chips away at the problem. Notice if or when answers bubble to the surface. Jot them down in your journal before they fly away.

⊙ Wishlist Walk: Do you have a Walk or Adventure that you've been wanting to embark on forever, but haven't made the time? There's a reason you've saved pictures of it and sighed every time a friend talks about this place. Find an excuse, whether it's a retreat, an art installation, or a seminar, make plans and go! Once there, let your heart decide what you want to see or do. Notice and journal the epiphanies and emotions that arise. What did you learn?

⊙ Labyrinth Walk: Labyrinth-walking is a wonderful way of walking into your truths. Use an online Labyrinth Locator to find one near you. As you wind in and out, notice what arises from within. Journal what comes up.

Buzzing with ideas or enjoyed an 'Intuition' activity recently? Record them below:

Journal This:

A place that deeply relaxes or delights you is often a portal to your inner wisdom. Make a list of these places for you so that you can turn to them when you need an Intuitive Soul Walk.

Think of some times in the past when inner wisdom and guidance bubble up to the surface when you least expect them. What were you doing at the time? Where were you?

Explorer's Notes

Related Cards:

How can you pair these related cards for a more interesting 'Intuition' wonder-walk?

Follow the Rabbit, Listen, Symbolism, Portals

Explorer's Notes

"Look out for the interesting entrances and openings that hint of a mysterious world beyond."

Explorer's Notes

Portals

An entry, a threshold, a gateway. Can you spot the hidden portals into wondrous worlds?

One of my favorite ways to invigorate a long hike or walk is to look for physical portals around me - a hole in the tree, a burrow in the ground, a hidden doorway - and then imagining what I'll see on the other side, if I'll catch a glimpse of a woodland nymph or wander into a dark, shadowy land full of mysterious creatures. As a truth-finding exercise, the 'Portals' walk has me examining entries, exits, thresholds and liminal spaces as personal metaphors for my life journey at the moment.

Interpretations:
The way in.
An opening to a secret world.
Door to the unknown.
A threshold between worlds.
Enter at your own risk.

Realm Symbolism:
Truth-Finding: The Inner Realm
Corresponding Symbolism: Water, Emotion, Feeling
Ask: What inner truths might a 'Portals' walk reveal?

Observe This on Your Wonder-Walk:

Look out for the interesting entrances and openings that hint of a mysterious world beyond: secret doorways in hedges; elaborate gates and arches in the middle of nowhere; interesting portholes and windows; concealed doors in unexpected places; archways and tunnels into the unknown; holes in trees, burrows in the ground...

Notice what portals are pulling at your curiosity and give yourself permission to step through them (if possible!) Examine how you feel when you allow yourself to indulge your curiosity and head into a mysterious unknown. Are any emotions emerging *e.g.* fear, discomfort, excitement, anticipation? Observe what you see and feel at the portal threshold, during the experience, as well as at the exit.

Activities to Try:

- ☉ The Portal Walk: Select a few Portals from your favorite fairy tales *(*<u>Alice in Wonderland</u>, <u>The Secret Garden</u>, <u>The Magic Faraway Tree</u>, *etc.)* and see if you can find them in your next Wonder-Walk.

- ☉ Imagining Portals: Paint or write a poem about what you imagine you'll see when you walk through the Portal. Let your imagination run wild!

- ☉ The Soul Walk: Before you begin your Portal Walk, think of a problem you'd like to untangle - *a creative block, a niggling issue at home or work.* Imagine the Portals you encounter on your walk as invitations to explore possibilities. *A magical doorway hidden in the hedge might be a hint that a delightful opportunity is right under your nose; a grand archway a sign that thinking bigger would be welcomed, etc.* Have fun, be open to answers in unexpected places!

Buzzing with ideas or enjoyed a 'Portal' activity recently? Record them below:

Journal This:

What can you leave behind at the Portal so that you can enter with heart and soul wide open?

Why did this Portal catch your eye?

What are some of your favorite Portals on your Wonder-Walks? What do they remind you of? (Anything from childhood, a story, an experience, a memory of a place?)

Explorer's Notes

Related Cards:

How can you pair these related cards for a more interesting 'Portal' wonder-walk?

Fairy Worlds, Pretend, Follow the Rabbit, Edges

Explorer's Notes

"There are few things more constant in my everyday life..."

Explorer's Notes

The Moon

Let the moon light your walk. Embrace the rhythmic, the enchanted, and the wisdom it reveals.

There are few things more constant in my everyday life than the moon, who has been with me through numerous houses and landscapes across three continents. It's been a giant comforting lantern in the sky, lighting my way through the dark and light of life's changes. It's been steadfast and rhythmic, a mysterious shimmering presence next to the sun's brilliance. No matter how many times I glimpse it rising above the horizon like a gold coin from a gossamer silk purse, it never ceases to fill me with wonder and awe. The moon speaks to me on so many levels - as the yin to the sun's yang, as the queen of nature's cycles and rhythms, as a gentle, ever-present anchor in the ephemeral journey of life.

Interpretations:
Nature's rhythms and cycles
Dependability, Constancy
Feminine, mystery, unknown
A subtle, soft light

Realm Symbolism:
Truth-Finding: The Inner Realm
Corresponding Symbolism: Water, Emotion, Feeling
Ask: What inner truths might a 'Moon' walk reveal?

Observe This on Your Wonder-Walk:

What does the shape of the moon remind you of tonight?
Do the different stages of the moon (full, waxing, waning, crescent, etc.) affect how you experience your walks? When does the moon appear bigger or smaller in the sky?

Observe how it feels to walk on a night lit by a fingernail moon versus a full moon. Observe the tides, the wildlife, the plants and fungi at different times of the month. Notice the moon shadows, how it lights up the land in different ways than the sun.

In all these walking scenarios, notice how it affects your feelings, moods and emotions.

Activities to Try:

⊙ The Full Moon Walk: There's something special about a full moon walk (with or without a loved one). It's bright enough to light up dark trails and turn the environment into a magical and haunting stage of shadows and silhouettes.
-Choose a wonder-walk that's away from light pollution, preferably in nature.
-Pack a flashlight and if desired, a small midnight picnic: a thermos of hot chocolate on a cold night, fruit, cake, a warm blanket.
-Challenge yourself to walk without any flashlight, stay quiet and respectful of nocturnal animals. Let the moon light your way. As you walk, release an intention or expectation into the night sky.
-Observe how the moon moves in the sky, how it makes you feel, and how moonlight (vs. sunlight) transforms your surroundings.
-Did you feel a yearning to connect to the other moon phases (new, waxing/waning) too? What rituals can you put in place to honor them?

⊙ Moon Effects: How does the moon affect the earth and its creatures? Plan a series of wonder-walks over a month to observe how the different phases of the moon influence the natural world:
-High and low tides (what are the repercussions?)
-Wildlife (especially nocturnal and tidal creatures)
-Plants (moon-planting: myth or fact?)
-Journal your discoveries and feelings about exploring the relationship moon has on life.

Buzzing with ideas or enjoyed a 'Moon' activity recently? Record them below:

Journal This:

What is your first memory of the moon? Can you remember? Go as far back as possible.

What does the moon mean to you? Why?

What feelings, emotions and truths emerged on your moon walk? Does it change with the moon cycles?

Explorer's Notes

Related Cards:

How can you pair these related cards for a more interesting 'Moon' wonder-walk?

Darkness, Symbolism, Shape, Poetry

Explorer's Notes

"It's thet sweet rush of affection, of sometimes unexplained familiarity, of the soul saying, yes *this*."

Explorer's Notes

Home

Ponder what places feel like home. Why?
Are homes intangible or concrete?

Is home where you're presently nesting, or the town you spent
most of childhood in? Is it that feeling when you first walked
into a bookstore, or the wondrous space itself? Having moved
around most of my life, home has become, sometimes out of the
need for constancy, a rightness of feeling deep inside. It's the
places I've laid down roots and made friends, but also the people
I've recognized as kindred spirits. It's the books and music that
mirror the ones inside me, but also the joy when a painting
turns out exactly right. Home is that sweet rush of affection, of
sometimes unexplained familiarity, of the soul saying, yes, *this*.

Interpretations:
Returning to the center, soul-aligned
A place we belong to; a dwelling
A rightness of feeling; when it all fits; meant to be
Where we've laid down roots or nested

Realm Symbolism:
Truth-Finding: The Inner Realm
Corresponding Symbolism: Water, Emotion, Feeling
Ask: What inner truths might a 'Home' walk reveal?

Observe This on Your Wonder-Walk:

Hold the feeling of home, that distinct, intuitive rightness,
just before your walk. Observe what evokes this feeling as you
walk. Have you always felt this way? Or is this something that
developed as you gradually made this environment your home?

As you walk, ponder what you're particularly fond of in your
surroundings. Perhaps it's important that you can walk or
cycle everywhere, or that your children are able to play safely
outdoors. Maybe it's being surrounded by trees or rolling hills.
What features and amenities make you feel like you belong here?
Notice the places that your soul feels deeply connected to, even
strangely familiar. Do you see anything that reminds you of
places you used to live?

Activities to Try:

⊙ **Home as a Place:** Wonder-walk somewhere in your home environment where you have a good view of the entire area. This is usually somewhere on higher ground - *on top of a hill, a viewing tower, a lighthouse, a rooftop, etc.* With gratitiude in your heart, survey this land you're calling home.
-Refer to the questions on the previous page about walking observations. Journal how you feel about living in this area and observe what elements make it feel especially like home. Ponder what you can do to feel even more at home here.
-Alternatively, wonder-walk and ponder these same questions in your house or yard.

⊙ **Home as a Feeling:** Head out for walk in town or an area where there is plenty of visual stimulation - *a main street, a library, a museum, an outdoor fair or market.* As you walk, make a note of the feeling of rightness - *e.g.* attraction, fondness, familiarity, as if you're being reunited with something or someone at soul level. Journal when this happens, and if it's meaningful in any way.

⊙ **Home as a Belonging:** Home is often where we feel like we're a part of something bigger. Wonder-walk somewhere local to you and ponder how home and belonging intertwine for you.
-Journal: What elements of a place or community make you feel especially welcomed, like you fit right in?
-Go deeper: refer to the section for the 'Belonging' card for more activity ideas for belonging to the land.

Buzzing with ideas or enjoyed a 'Home' activity recently? Record them below:

Journal This:

What does home mean to you? Describe your feelings and thoughts around the idea of home.

What are some of your fondest memories of home in childhood? Why do you think it's memorable?

Is there anything you're feeling a little lost about and would like to return 'home' to?

Explorer's Notes

Related Cards:

How can you pair these related cards for a more interesting 'Home' wonder-walk?

Memory, Belonging, Roots, Journey

Explorer's Notes

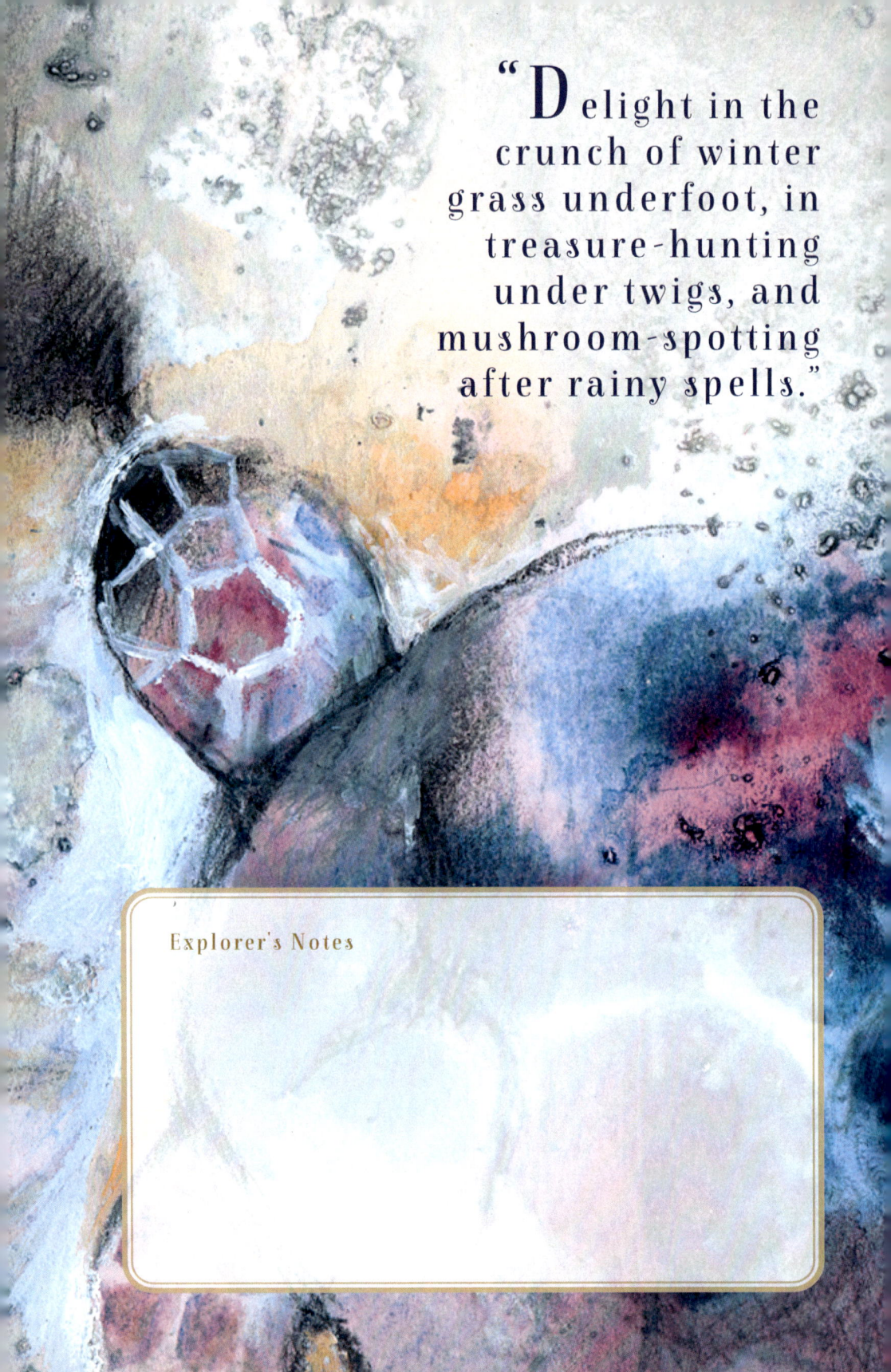

"**D**elight in the crunch of winter grass underfoot, in treasure-hunting under twigs, and mushroom-spotting after rainy spells."

Explorer's Notes

Wonder

An amazement, an inquiry, a marveling.
Wander in wonder and let enchantment lead the way.

Wonder is my 6-year-old niece poking at caterpillars and gasping with delight at a brand new box of toy mice. Wonder is both the swelling feeling in my chest at my first wildflower superbloom, as well as the curiosity that arises every time I look up into a starry night sky. Wonder is that intoxicating sense of rapture and reverence we naturally had as children, a state that gradually fades in adulthood. This card invites us to be child-like again, to see the world as if we've never seen it before, mysterious and magical, full of marvelous possibilities lying in wait around every corner.

Interpretations:
Amazement, rapture, reverence
Child-like perception, seeing with fresh eyes
Sheer and utter delight
Curiosity, inquiry, to puzzle over
Everyday magic and delight

Realm Symbolism:
Truth-Finding: The Inner Realm
Corresponding Symbolism: Water, Emotion, Feeling
Ask: What inner truths might a 'Wonder' walk reveal?

Observe This on Your Wonder-Walk:

Walk a place as if you've never been there before, new and fresh and full of hidden splendors. Delight in the crunch of winter grass underfoot, in treasure-hunting under twigs, and mushroom-spotting after rainy spells.

Explore like the child you once were, curious about the smallest miracles around you - the shimmering iridescence inside an abalone shell, windswept cypress trees along the coast, the misty puff of one's breath on a cold morning.

Give yourself permission to ask 'silly' questions and be awe-struck by the most ordinary of happenings around you.

Activities to Try:

- Favorite Wonder-Walks: While all of the cards in this deck (and book) will awaken wonder when in use, it's not unusual for some of the cards to provide an easier path to magic than others. Here are my favorites: *Pretend, Follow the Rabbit, Naiveté, Fairy Worlds, Portals, Enchantment*. Start with these cards, but feel free to choose your own set as you get to know them. Experiment with their recommended activities and journal the card(s) that inspire rapture and curiosity the easiest.

- Magic in the Everyday: This is a simple activity of noticing everyday wonders that delight your inner child. This can be carried out indoors at home, or outdoors in nature or an urban environment.
  -Indoors (at home): *E.g. running water, central heating, fresh laundry, baking cookies in the oven, a lit candle.* Think about a time where modern luxuries didn't exist.
  -Outdoors: *E.g. raindrops on puddles, eroded holes in beach pebbles, a field of flowers, ocean waves.* Journal the emotions that arise in these two scenarios above. What do you find wondrous about them? Is this meaningful in any way?
  -Creative challenge: record short films of these magical (indoor or outdoor) moments on your phone or camera to celebrate them.

Buzzing with ideas or enjoyed a 'Wonder' activity recently? Record them below:

Journal This:

What is your favorite kind of wonder-walk? Describe what easily inspires rapture and curiosity. Why?

What simple everyday pleasures and delights did you notice around your house or yard? How is this meaningful?

What wonder rituals would you incorporate into your everyday to notice and celebrate the simple miracles in life?

Explorer's Notes

Related Cards:

How can you pair these related cards for a more interesting 'Wonder' wonder-walk?

Naiveté, Enchantment, Fairy Worlds, Thumbelina

Explorer's Notes

"My soul is whispering where to walk and I am ensorcelled..."

Explorer's Notes

Listen

Listen, not just to the soundscapes, but what arises from within when your body relaxes into the land.

Some days, it's as if a door to my soul has flung wide open and every walk, sight, and experience is a path straight to the heart. I become a magnet for magic, like a plant in the desert soaking up water. The greens of leaves are greener, the flowing river more sparkling, the birdsong sweeter. I treasure such magical moments, for they are dialogues with my inner self, opportunities to fill my spirit cup. My soul whispers where to walk and I am ensorcelled. Aliveness tingles from the top of my head to the tips of my toes. And so I am alert to the inner call for conversation, and when it comes, I know to seek the places of quiet solitude in which to hear these whispers from within.

Interpretations:
A dialogue with the inner self
A need for stillness. quiet and solitude
To go within, listen to intuition
To notice or pay attention

Realm Symbolism:
Truth-Finding: The Inner Realm
Corresponding Symbolism: Water, Emotion, Feeling
Ask: What inner truths might a 'Listen' walk reveal?

Observe This on Your Wonder-Walk:

This walk is about finding or creating the stillness needed to tune into your inner wisdom. Often it means being out when or where other humans aren't - on the beach at dawn, up a hill in the crepescule hours, strolling or roaming your neighborhood streets at night. As you walk, observe when and where peace begins for you. Notice when distraction and noise melt away and your inner voice bubbles up easily from within.

Sometimes stillness can be found amidst the roar of activity when no one is paying attention to you - in the din of a bustling city square, amidst the cacophany of an ocean feeding frenzy, during a rumbling thunderstorm. Pay attention to moments when your body relaxes into the experience and begins listening.

Activities to Try:

⊙ The Stillness Walk: Choose a location to walk that's pleasing, comfortable and peaceful. Leave all electronics at home. If possible, choose a walk that unfolds like a journey, *e.g. begins at a path through the forest, passes a river, crosses a bridge, culminates at a scenic overlook.* This provides a stimulating change of scenery that invites relaxation, slowing down, and attunement of your senses to your surroundings. It's also the perfect condition for wisdom to rise from within.
-Before you begin, prepare a Beautiful Inquiry to ponder while you walk. *This can be a problem at work, a vision for a creative project, or a personal pain to work through.*
-Begin walking, relax into the land, slow down.
-Turn off your mind and let your senses soak in the beautiful sights, sounds, smells.
-If it comes up, gently allow your mind to contemplate your Beautiful Inquiry in the background as you walk. Can you hear yourself think? If not, keep bringing your attention back to your surroundings. Strive for utter relaxation and stillness, and often answers will come.

⊙ Yin / Yang Walk: A Yin (feminine) walk is receptive in nature, a 'stillness' meandering type of walk that's often about savoring the journey. A Yang (masculine) walk is driven, challenging, goal-oriented. Which walk is best for you today?

Buzzing with ideas or enjoyed a 'Listen' activity recently? Record them below:

Journal This:

What am I hearing but not really listening to right now?

When do you usually feel the need to listen to your inner self?
Why do you think this happens?

Where do you usually go to tune into the wisdom within?
Describe this place and how it helps you relax and be at peace.

Explorer's Notes

Related Cards:

How can you pair these related cards for a more
interesting 'Listen' wonder-walk?

Notice, Intuition, Immersion, Dawn

Explorer's Notes

"If we choose to enter the land of shadows, all is not doomed, for our eyes adjust and a magical nocturnal world opens up before us."

Explorer's Notes

Darkness

Darkness is the absence of light; but also when it's most needed." What do you see when your eyes adjust?

A walk in darkness is a confronting of old fears - a fear of the dark woods; a fear of the murky ocean floor where unseen creatures lay await; a fear of what we don't know. And yet, darkness is when the contrast of light is its most glorious, like the wonder of a starry night sky, joyful fairy lights at a wedding soirée, the mystical pale sliver of a crescent moon. If we choose to enter the land of shadows, all is not doomed, for our eyes adjust and soon a nocturnal world, mysterious and magical, opens up before us. What will we see when our shadowy veil melts away?

Interpretations:
An absence of light
Nocturne; of the night
Umbra, shadow, gloom
Unilluminated, unenlightened
Unknown or unseen

Realm Symbolism:
Truth-Finding: The Inner Realm
Corresponding Symbolism: Water, Emotion, Feeling
Ask: What inner truths might a walk in 'Darkness reveal?

Observe This on Your Wonder-Walk:

Darkness comes in all shapes and forms. Some are shadowy crevices and caves in rocks. Some are dark man-made tunnels and dense forests. Others are gloomy depths like the lakes and oceans. And then there is the darkness that blankets all the land when the sun sinks into the horizon.

What are some of your favorite darkened places to walk?

Notice what you're most intrigued by or are afraid of. Which part of you is on alert in the dark? Is your sense of hearing sharper; what do you hear? Most of all, savor the magical feeling of sight when your eyes adjust to the inkiness.

Activities to Try:

⊙ Solo Camping Trip: There's nothing like a solo camping trip in nature to brings out all shades of darkness - setting up our tent at dusk; the pitch black of a night spent in the wild away from city lights; wonder-walks at midnight lit by twinkling stars; being alone with our thoughts, doubts, and fears. There's no running away, and that is the beauty of the experience. Practice savoring the darkness and all it unveils, within and without. Journal any epiphanies.

⊙ A Nature Walk In the Dark: If you can't get away for a solo camping trip, plan a moonlit or starry night wonder-walk with a friend or loved one. Journal what you notice and how you felt as your eyes adjusted to the darkness.

⊙ Eucatastrophe: J.R.R Tolkien talks about the concept of *eucatastrophe* in fairy tales - a period of darkness followed by the piercing joy of light and how the contrast makes it more meaningful. Can you think of some experiences that are made more magical because of the dark? *A nighttime light installation at the local park; Edgar Allan Poe readings lit by candlelight; a camera obscura room at a museum.* Plan a trip to such an event. Journal the wonder and how the experience feels during and after.

Buzzing with ideas or enjoyed a 'Darkness' activity recently? Record them below:

Journal This:

What are some shadowy physical places you're afraid to walk? Is it the haunted house on Halloween? The woods after sunset?

Relate this to your fears and the unexplored sides of your self.

What are some wonderful physical experiences (the fireworks, a light show, etc.) you've had recently or in the past that can only happen because of darkness?

Relate this to a problem you're working through right now.

Explorer's Notes

Related Cards:

How can you pair these related cards for a more interesting wonder-walk in 'Darkness'?

Dusk, Hidden, Discomfort, The Woods

Explorer's Notes

"**P**erhaps it's the softness of everything that blurs the line between real and unreal."

Explorer's Notes

Fog

Fog is a feeling. An atmosphere. A dream.
How does it make you feel in it?

There is something about being enveloped in a blanket of
white fog that instantly transports me to faraway dream
worlds. Perhaps it's the softness of everything that blurs
the line between real and unreal. Perhaps it's because the
mythical and fairy stories of my childhood have always taken
place in misty, foggy lands. But fog to me is also more than
just an atmosphere. It's that feeling of being cocooned in a
haze of inspiration, often during an intense period of focused
activity or contemplation. What does fog mean to you?

Interpretations:
In a bubble or cocoon.
Melancholy, moody.
A state of befuddlement.
Ethereal and dream-like.
Obscurity, mystification, veiled.

Realm Symbolism:
Truth-Finding: The Inner Realm
Corresponding Symbolism: Water, Emotion, Feeling
Ask: What inner truths might a 'Fog' walk reveal?

Observe This on Your Wonder-Walk:

If you're lucky enough to live where the mist or fog rolls in
at sunrise or sunset (or any other time), notice how it makes
you feel when you walk in it. Do you feel differently when it's
thicker or thinner?

Does the softening and obscuring of your environment delight
or discombobulate you? How far can you see? What kind of
worlds can you imagine beyond the veil of gray-white?

Pretend the shapes obscured by fog are not what they are in
reality. A tree could be a giant sloth. A fire tower, perhaps a
castle in a fairy tale. Let your imagination run wild!

Activities to Try:

⊙ The Fog Walk: Select one of these foggy experiences - *a walk in the misty or foggy outdoors, a trip to a steam room at a local spa, an outdoor hot springs in the dead of winter.*

Observe how you feel when your surroundings fade away. Do you feel more or less in tune with yourself? Are you able to hear your inner voice clearer, or is the steam or fog distracting? What feelings are coming up?

⊙ A Foggy Movie: The next time you watch a movie with a foggy scene, notice how it makes you feel. What emotion is the director and cinematographer hoping to evoke by setting the scene in a foggy locale? How is this important to the storyline?

⊙ Imagining Fog: Look through old magazines or Pinterest for beautiful, foggy pictures - *misty mountains or forests, mist over lakes and rivers, a foggy beach, etc.* What do these pictures make you think of? Why?

Buzzing with ideas or enjoyed a 'Fog' activity recently? Record them below:

Journal This:

Describe how it felt when you were walking through the fog or mist. Did you imagine dreamy worlds or creatures on your foggy walk? Where do you think these images came from?

When was the last time you felt enveloped in a haze where time stood still and your surrounding world faded away? What were you doing at the time?

Are there any similarities between an actual foggy walk and a mental fog experience?

Explorer's Notes

Related Cards:

How can you pair these related cards for a more interesting 'Fog' wonder-walk?

Dream, Fairy Worlds, Pretend, Memory

Explorer's Notes

"Change is imminent, and the body and soul knows it."

Explorer's Notes

Edges

*On the edges of places come a change, a boundary, a transition.
When do you cross from one to another?*

I've always been fascinated with edges - knowing where they are,
finding ways to mark them, learning how to push them. I believe
that edges of places and experiences are where the most glorious
things happen. The land transforms as it approaches the ocean, just
as do we when we straddle the thresholds of life between now and
what's next. Change is imminent, and the body and soul knows it.
An edge is a cusp, a transition, a rich liminal space teaming with
life, like the tidepools and estuaries of the world. It is a boundary,
a place of endings and beginnings, the deep breath before the
plunge. What happens when you cross over?

Interpretations:
In-between place or state
A liminal space
Boundary, demarcation, limits
Cusp, transition, change
Threshold, gateway, doorway

Realm Symbolism:
Truth-Finding: The Inner Realm
Corresponding Symbolism: Water, Emotion, Feeling
Ask: What inner truths might an 'Edges' walk reveal?

Observe This on Your Wonder-Walk:

Notice the edges on your walks - when one place becomes another
or when two places merge and form a new in-between place. What
are some physical characteristics of edges? Are they natural or
man-made? Recent or formed over millions of years?

What happens at edges when land becomes sea or meadow becomes
forest? What wildlife and plants make these in-between places
their home? Notice the gates, the fences, the statelines, the city
boundaries. Can you tell when you're exiting one and entering
another?

Notice the edges of the day, when light becomes dark and all that
comes alive. How do changes in your surroundings make you feel?

Activities to Try:

⊙ A Liminal Excursion: Spend a few hours at an in-between place. *Some ideas to try: river banks, coastal woodlands, tide pools, estuaries, foothills or valleys. Try also, porches and foyers of historic homes or buildings.*

Journal or sketch what you see and how you feel as you cross from one place to another. Is there a clear demarcation? Is there anything special or unique to that transitional place? Notice the people, wildlife and plants that frequent or inhabit them. What activities take place? Compare how you feel when you're in one place, when you're transitioning, and when you've crossed over to the other place.

⊙ Pushing Your Edges: The purpose of this activity is to push what you believe are your physical or mental boundaries. Just like an octopus squeezing through an inconceivably tiny crevice in the reef, we may surprise ourselves by redefining the limits we've placed around what's possible.

Select an activity just outside your comfort zone - if you normally walk for 1 mile, try doing it uphill, or walking 2 miles. If you've never traveled alone, maybe plan a day trip to a nearby town by yourself. Journal how it feels when what you think is a limit or boundary dissolves.

Buzzing with ideas or enjoyed an 'Edges' activity recently? Record them below:

Journal This:

Describe a point in your life when you spent some time at the transitional edge of something new. What did it feel like? Relate this to a physical edge or liminal space you encountered on a wonder-walk recently.

What are some of your favorite liminal places, thresholds or edges you've visited? Why?

Have you ever felt trapped in an in-between place? What do you do to complete the crossing?

Explorer's Notes

Related Cards:

How can you pair these related cards for a more interesting 'Edges' wonder-walk?

Portals, Connect, Discomfort, Symbolism

Explorer's Notes

Indulge your curiosity.

Secret Garden

The Influence Realm

"The sun invites me to examine my relationship with light."

The Sun

The sun brings clarity, awakening, illumination.
What needs to be enlightened as you walk?

Growing up in the hot and humid tropics and spending most
of my adulthood in the searing heat of Western Australia and
Southern California meant that I had to learn to navigate my
complex relationship with the sun - when I look forward to
it, when I don't, when I appreciate it the most. A friend in
painting and photography, inspiringly glorious at twilight,
a warm comfort in cool, rainy months, a source of magic
dappled in a forest or diffused through evening mists - the
sun invites me to examine my relationship with light and how
it influences my actions and sense of aliveness.

Interpretations:
Clarity or illumination
A source of warmth
Masculine, active energy
Bold, brilliant, dazzling

Realm Symbolism:
Secret Garden: The Influence Realm
Corresponding Symbolism: Air, Intellect, Thinking
Ask: How does the 'Sun' influence your walk?

Observe This on Your Wonder-Walk:

Observe how the sun influences your perception of your
surroundings at different times of the day. The same walk can
be stark under the noonday sun but magical at sunset and
even haunting in the blue hours of twilight.

Notice when the sun feels the most welcome and when it's not.
Observe how it illuminates the world around you in different
ways, the patterns and textures it creates. What do you tend to
notice or miss depending on the position of the sun and time
of day?

Wonder-walk like an Impressionist painter - paying attention
to the way sunlight reacts with atmosphere to reveal hidden
colors and optical effects - reflected, refracted, scattered.

Activities to Try:

⊙ The Sun Map: Select your favorite place to wonder-walk, somewhere accessible at different times of the day.
-In your journal, map out the times of the day where light differs dramatically. *e.g. Dawn, Noon, Dusk, Night.*
-Visit and walk your chosen place at these times within the same day or season.
-Observe and record how the different sun positions and interactions with atmospheric changes influence your mood, experience and activities.
-Journal, photograph or paint the same spot at these different times and compare them side by side, noting what thoughts and feelings emerge.

⊙ Magic in Optical Effects: Vibrant and colorful displays occur when sunlight interacts with the tiny particles in our atmosphere - *rainbows, haloes, rays, iridescence, etc.* Reflected, refracted, and scattered by water droplets, ice crystals or dust particles, sunlight becomes a whimsical and magical theater for the imagination. Record, photograph or sketch whenever you witness these phenomena on your wonder-walks.

⊙ Instruments of Wonder: Bring along a piece of frosted acrylic, a magnifying glass, a handmade paper pinhole camera, a faceted crystal, a kaleidoscope or a telescope on your next wonder-walk. Experiment with how these instruments reflect, diffuse and interact with sunlight to create wondrous effects. Write a poem, paint or photograph your discoveries.

Buzzing with ideas or enjoyed a 'Sun' activity recently? Record them below:

Journal This:

What quality of natural light do you enjoy the most? Warm and sunny? Ethereal and diffused? Dappled and reflected? At what time of the day? Why?

How does this influence the places and wonder-walks you choose to explore? Why?

What would you like the 'sun' to illuminate right now?

Explorer's Notes

Related Cards:

How can you pair these related cards for a more interesting 'Sun' Wonder-Walk?

Dawn, Dusk, Color, Fairy Worlds

Explorer's Notes

"To walk as a poet is to be bravely sentimental, deeply inquisitive, unflinchingly awake."

Explorer's Notes

Poetry

Feel deeply, unleash the inner poet.
Let yourself be figurative, symbolic and lyrical on your walk.

A poetic walk invites us to form a sharp, intimate knowing
of our surroundings. An effortless lyricism that can only be
born from fierce, passionate attention to all the world around
us, from the mundane to the glorious. Emotion is our secret
weapon; the heart, our guide. For me, to walk as a poet is to be
bravely sentimental, deeply inquisitive, unflinchingly awake.
Just as we need not wait for something to happen before we
can write it, paint it, or photograph it, a simple, everyday walk
need not be resplendent with rainbows and red sunsets to
render it sublime poetry.

Interpretations:
Magic in the ordinary
Sensitive, heartfelt expression
Brevity, irreducibility; achieving much with little
Romantic, sentimental view

Realm Symbolism:
Secret Garden: The Influence Realm
Corresponding Symbolism: Air, Intellect, Thinking
Ask: How would 'Poetry' influence your walk?

Observe This on Your Wonder-Walk:

Walk as if you were a poet. Observe your surroundings for
images and impressions to inspire your passionate artist
heart. Pay attention to the everyday quiet of small things -
find the splendor in summer's blade of grass; wonder in early
morning frost on wildflowers; rapture over raindrops rippling
in rhythm over a tidal pond.

Allow yourself to be unabashedly romantic in your
perceptions, experiment with words and similes to describe
what you see - *sunlight bouncing off the water like strings of
scattered diamonds.* Play with metaphor to connect how you
feel with what your senses take in. Notice the poetry of place -
the intimate details that make up a magical whole.

Activities to Try:

⊙ A Wonder-Walk Poem: Write a poem about your wonder-walk.
  -Begin it with "I see...", or select another card from this Wonder-Walking Deck to inspire the poem. *Fauna*, *Flora*, *Fairy Worlds* are fun ones. Try also, *Moon*, *Dawn* or *Dusk*.
  -Distill what you've experienced; be concise.
  -Be richly detailed in your choice of words so that the reader would feel right there with you - describe the textures, colors, atmosphere. Sink into the five senses.
  -Don't be afraid to infuse emotion and feelings through play on words, allegory or metaphor.

⊙ Poetry in Study: Study your favorite poets, particularly those that write vividly about their nature or exterior world experiences. Mary Oliver, Robert Frost, and Wendell Berry are some easy ones to start with. Observe how they use poetry to describe their connection with the exterior world, and sometimes, how it mirrors their interior life.

  Alternatively, study books on poetry-writing like the <u>The Poet's Companion</u> or <u>The Triggering Town</u> (*see* Bibliography for more details). You'll find wonderful exercises on observation and writing that would help make your wonder-walks more deeply engaging.

Buzzing with ideas or enjoyed a 'Poetry' activity recently? Record them below:

Journal This:

What is your favorite poem of all time? Why?

How is your favorite poem evocative of your inner or exterior world right now?

What words do you usually find yourself using to describe your wonder-walking experiences when journaling? Do you see a pattern in the way you express yourself? In your preference for a particular mood or atmosphere?

Explorer's Notes

Related Cards:

How can you pair these related cards for a more interesting 'Poetry' Wonder-Walk?

Mood Painting, Notice, Symbolism, Thumbelina

Explorer's Notes

"**W**hy am I here
in this very place
right now?"

Explorer's Notes

Journey

Journeys past and present intersect in place. Let your walk reveal where you've been and where you're going.

We belong to the land, and the land belongs to us. Our journeys intertwine inevitably as the seasons, landscape and weather shape the decisions we make about what we leave behind, where we are and how we'd like our lives to unfold. All the places I've called home live inside me, become a part of my story and infuses my dreams and goals. The spirit of place imprints itself into my soul and I am always changed by the roots I put down. This wonder-walk asks: why am I here in this very place right now? What does the the land have to teach me about myself and my journey at this moment? What do I have to give to it?

Interpretations:
Voyage, odyssey, passage, adventure
Process of getting from one point to another
Stages of life, milestones
Mythology, saga, tale

Realm Symbolism:
Secret Garden: The Influence Realm
Corresponding Symbolism: Air, Intellect, Thinking
Ask: What would enhance your 'Journey' walk?

Observe This on Your Wonder-Walk:

As you walk, pay attention to surrounding elements that synchronize with your journey, past, present or future. Notice if it contrasts with where you were living before, and what messages, if any, it holds about where you'd like to go next. Are you being drawn to any particular feature - the hills, the ocean, the historic buildings? Perhaps, like me, you've dreamed of labyrinths for years, only to unexpectedly move right next to one!

Living by the ocean makes one sensitive to the moon and its tidal repercussions. California hills herald the hiking season when they transform from the scorched brown of drought into the green of spring. Notice if anything feels particularly poignant because it's influenced your everyday thoughts, activities and emotions.

Activities to Try:

⊙ A Journey Mindmap: Create a mindmap of your life journey through the different places you've lived in to explore connections between the two.
   -On a large sheet of paper or in your journal, drawn a line dividing the page in two. On the top half, draw a series of bubbles to represent important milestones in your life. Fill in the bubbles.
   -On the bottom half of the paper, in corresponding bubbles, draw or write where you were living at the time. Write a short paragraph to describe this place, *e.g. "Green wooden house on top of the hill surrounded by oak trees", "Peach house 3 bus stops away from the ocean and a small town full of magic shops."*
   -Draw a line to connect the place and event bubbles. In the space between the two, write any connections you find between life events and the places you've lived. Journal the epiphanies.
   -Wonder-walk these old haunts if you can. How do you feel about them right now?

⊙ Right Here, Right Now: Draw or paint a map of where you live right now. Fill in your favorite wonder-walk places. Make them yours by naming them in intimate, whimsical ways: *"The Fairy Tree", "The Disappearing Beach"*. Are there any correspondences between your favorite places and your current life goals, interests and pursuits? Make a note of them on the map. Have fun: make it a creative project! Collage, paint, stitch: no rules.

Buzzing with ideas or enjoyed a 'Journey' activity recently? Record them below:

Journal This:

Where have you rooted in the past that felt particularly important to your journey at the time? Describe the landscape, the experience of living there, and how it intersected your dreams and pursuits in a significant way.

Why do you think you're living where you are right now? What are some of your favorite haunts and walks? How does it mirror your journey at this moment?

Related Cards:

How can you pair these related cards for a more interesting 'Journey' Wonder-Walk?

Belonging, Roots, Home, Spirit of Place

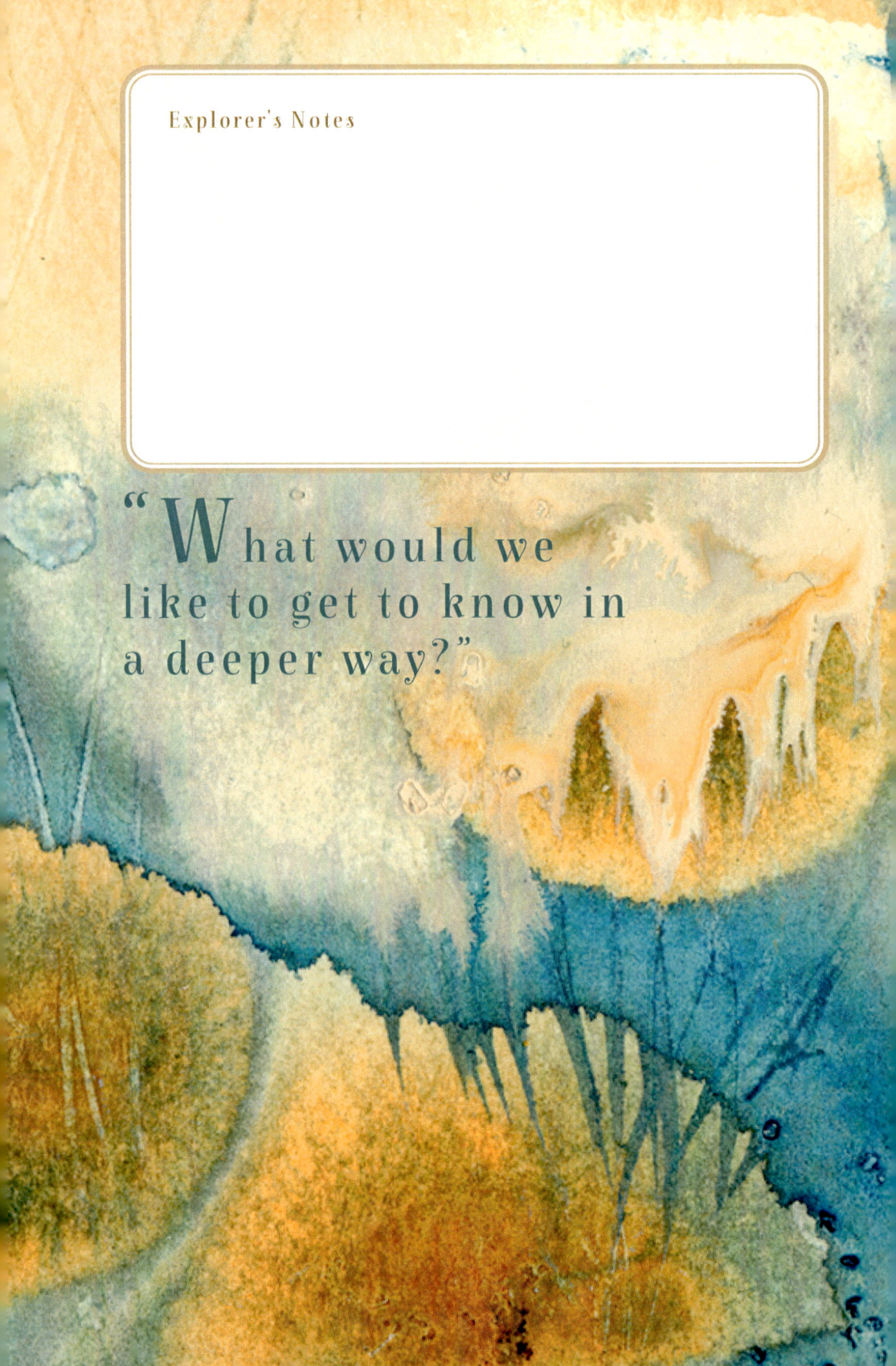

"What would we like to get to know in a deeper way?"

Study

Examine, explore, analyze with intention.
How will your walk be enriched by study?

Have you ever noticed that the world around us becomes infinitely more alive, fascinating, and meaningful the more we know about it? To immerse ourselves in knowledge of a place - its history, inhabitants and stories - is to know it, understand it, connect with it. We become so attuned to its idiosyncrasies, to the minutae of familiarity, that a kind of kinship forms, no matter if it's a tree, a house, the stormy ocean. This card asks: what are we drawn to studying around us? What would we like to get to know in a deeper way? How would it change us?

Interpretations:
Analyze or examine in detail
Explore, investigate, discover
To understand or empathize with
A deep acquaintance

Realm Symbolism:
Secret Garden: The Influence Realm
Corresponding Symbolism: Air, Intellect, Thinking
Ask: How would 'study' enhance your walk?

Observe This on Your Wonder-Walk:

Walk through the eyes of a naturalist or a 19th-century explorer on freshly discovered land, teeming with never-before-seen wonders. Bring a notebook along to record details and observations of what you find most fascinating around you.

Indulge your curiosity. Poke around rocks. Examine leaves and seed pods. Sketch. Refer to field guides. Ask Beautiful Inquiries about what you see around you: *Why does this particular eucalyptus tree grow sideways compared to the others? Why do sea figs turn orange?*

As you walk, select a subject to examine in the field and research later - the textures of various tree bark, the significance of historic Chinatown signs, edible local seaweed.

Activities to Try:

Knowing And Not-Knowing: Explore how information (or its absence) of a place influences the way you experience it.

Knowing: Plan a trip to a nearby monument or a cultural or historic landmark.
-Before you visit the place, read up on its history and significance to the area around it.
-Wonder-walk the place with this knowledge.
-Allow yourself to imagine what happened there in years past, and the people and events that shaped it through time, based on what you've studied.
-Record how having this information beforehand colors your experience of the place. Does it help you engage the place more vividly? Does prior knowledge make it more, or less, real to you?

Not-Knowing: Plan a trip to a similar place without knowing anything about it. Look at it through fresh eyes, examine and study anything that catches your eye on-site. Record what you find most fascinating and guess what might have happened based on firsthand observations. Ask who, what, why, and how questions during your wonder-walk.

Compare how knowing versus not-knowing changes your experience or enjoyment of places. Which do you prefer?

Buzzing with ideas or enjoyed a 'Study' activity recently? Record them below:

Journal This:

What are you drawn to on your walks recently that you've been itching to study and understand in a deeper way?

Can you think of a time when knowing more about a place you've visited makes the experience more vivid and/or haunting?

Why do you think you're fascinated by your chosen subject of study? What does it mean to your journey right now?

Explorer's Notes

Related Cards:

How can you pair these related cards for a more interesting 'Study' Wonder-Walk?

Flora, Fauna, Naiveté, Follow the Rabbit

Explorer's Notes

"Does walking in someone else's shoes transform the way you experience the world?"

Explorer's Notes

Pretend

Play dress up, slip on an alternate lens, try it on for size.
How can pretending color your walk today?

'Pretend' is a controversial word. To me it's like trying
something on for size - a little more playing dress-up and
putting on Mom's high heels, and less like fooling others.
On my 'Pretend' wonder walks, I let my imagination run as
wild as a child's, asking myself what I would notice if I was an
owl flying in the night, Mary Oliver on a sweet spring day, Van
Gogh in a creative frenzy. I conjure up enchanted forests in
ordinary woodlands, and make up stories about what I notice
around me.

Interpretations:
Looking through someone else's lens.
Walking in others' shoes.
Masquerade.
Imagine or conjure.
Dramatize.

Realm Symbolism:
Secret Garden: The Influence Realm
Corresponding Symbolism: Air, Intellect, Thinking
Ask: How would 'Pretending' enhance your walk?

Observe This on Your Wonder-Walk:

Notice what you tend to transform in your environments
during a 'Pretend' walk. Do you like to imagine trees as
teeming with fairy folk? Are doors in hedges always gateways
to magical worlds beyond?

Observe what features on your walk fade away or become
sharper when you slip on an alternate lens.

If you're walking a familiar route, what are you noticing that
you didn't before? Does anything look or feel different?
If you're wearing costumes or carrying yourself in an unusual
manner, how are people responding to you?

Activities to Try:

- Child's Play: Observe a five- or six-year-old at play. This could be your child (or a friend's), a niece or nephew, or a child in a video documentary. Notice how they diligently study the world around them and use their observations in their play. Do they transform a walk in the zoo into an imaginative fight between a tiger and an elephant? Does an evening roam in the tidepools translate to fantastical bathtub play?

  What are some interesting interpretations that you can borrow for your own wonder-walks? How can you learn to pretend again?

- The Pretend Walk: Select a favorite book or poem from childhood - *fairy stories or adventure and heroic journey tales are great choices* - and go on a wonder-walk pretending you're the main character. Does walking in someone else's shoes transform the way you experience the world?

  Try the above activity with favorite movies - *Lord of the Rings, Pan's Labyrinth, Star Wars,* etc. Give yourself permission to be silly!

- Poet for the Day: Pretend to be your favorite poet, author, artist for the duration of a walk, take field notes.

Buzzing with ideas or enjoyed a 'Pretend' activity recently? Record them below:

Journal This:

What are some of your best memories of pretending as a child? Start the page with "I used to..."

Describe the book/movie/artist 'Pretend' walk you went on. What did you notice or experience differently by wearing an alternate lens?

Make a list of writers, poets, artists you'd like to pretend to be for a day. Include book or movie characters, too.

Explorer's Notes

Related Cards:

How can you pair these related cards for a more interesting 'Pretend' Wonder-Walk?

Memory, Story, Fairy Worlds, Study

Explorer's Notes

"There is a strange kind of familiarity, a peculiar feeling of déjà vu, a sense of coming home."

Explorer's Notes

Connect

Stories, perceptions, history and land crisscross in an eternal web. What do you connect with?

There are places that I have lived or walked that felt like soul places, enveloping me in a warm embrace like old friends saying hello. There is a strange kind of familiarity, a peculiar feeling of déjà vu, a sense of coming home. It may as simple as a tree shaped like my sanctuary from childhood, or a complex scene straight out of a favorite fairy tale. Whatever shape this kinship takes, the questions remain: why do we connect to certain elements and places in our exterior world? Where do these feelings come from? Are they real or imagined? What are the threads that bind us in this tapestry of life?

Interpretations:
Kinship, bond, friendship
To relate, feel close to, or resonate with
A sense of belonging
Interwoven or intermingled

Realm Symbolism:
Secret Garden: The Influence Realm
Corresponding Symbolism: Air, Intellect, Thinking
Ask: What do you 'Connect' with on your walk?

Observe This on Your Wonder-Walk:

As you saunter through your surroundings, pay attention to what you feel connected to. It could be a physical trait of the land, a place history, a flower. It could be the morning mist encircling the green hills in just the way that reminds you of home. Observe how and why things are resonating.

Notice also if you feel connected to different things at different times as your mood, interests and pre-occupations shift through the days and seasons.

Observe if there's a pattern to the elements you're continually drawn to. A sailboat out in water. The craftsman bungalows in town. Explore the significance, and notice if these patterns symbolize a message you're needing to hear right now.

Activities to Try:

⊙ Rituals for Connecting to Place: Create a grounding ritual to connect to a new or favorite place. This is particularly helpful when visiting a new area for vacation, or when you've been away from your usual haunts for awhile.

Here are some ideas:
- Take off your shoes and walk or run barefoot.
- Dip your feet in a body of water - river, pond, ocean.
- Plan an outdoor picnic - solo or with a loved one.
- Rent or ride a bicycle to explore the area.
- Find a labyrinth to walk: https://labyrinthlocator.com/
- Visit the local botanical garden to get to know, or reconnect with, the area's native plants.
- Paint it, photograph it, write about it.
- Meditate in the place for 5-10 minutes at least.
- Visit a local farmers market to see what grows in the area, and to meet the folks that grow them.
- Visit a local natural history museum to understand the local ecosystems.

⊙ The Connection Game:

A: On a large piece of paper or in your journal pages, draw some bubbles. Write in each bubble elements that you connected with on a recent wonder-walk.

B: With a different colored pen or pencil, draw more bubbles containing your latest creative ideas, projects or interests.

- Connect A bubbles with B bubbles in unexpected combinations to spark interesting new ideas.

Buzzing with ideas or enjoyed a 'Connect' activity recently? Record them below:

Journal This:

What do you feel most connected to in the environment where you live right now? Why?

Can you recall when this connection might have begun? What does it remind you of? How is this significant?

What are some ways that you connect with a place, whether it's somewhere you walk everyday, or a new place you're just visiting? What makes you feel closer to the land?

Explorer's Notes

Related Cards:

How can you pair these related cards for a more interesting 'Connect' Wonder-Walk?

Memory, Synesthesia, Home, Belonging

Explorer's Notes

"Let your fascination guide you into untrodden territories."

Explorer's Notes

Follow the Rabbit

Explore, investigate probe. What will you discover if you followed the rabbit of curiosity?

In one of my favorite books from childhood, <u>Alice in Wonderland</u>, a little girl named Alice follows a frantic white rabbit through a dark hole and tumbles into an enchanted world beyond her imagination. This card invites us to indulge our own curiosity rabbits and lose ourselves in mystery and uncertainty. It asks us to examine, what lies beyond the boundaries of our comfort bubbles? How can we let go and surrender ourselves to our inquiring minds? Where would it lead us, what will we learn? How will our discoveries change us?

Interpretations:
Curiosity, inquisitiveness
Explorer spirit, investigator
To head into the unknown
A compelling lead, breadcrumb trail
Comfort in uncertainty

Realm Symbolism:
Secret Garden: The Influence Realm
Corresponding Symbolism: Air, Intellect, Thinking
Ask: What would you discover if you 'Followed the Rabbit?'

Observe This on Your Wonder-Walk:

Indulge your curious mind on your wonder-walk. Sniff, poke, and follow the breadcrumb trail of interest. Walk into that miniature dollhouse shop you've been wondering about every time you drive by. Cycle the trail you're hoping might connect to the other side of town but haven't had a chance to explore. Check out that enigmatic corner cafe with the delicious smells wafting out.

As you walk, notice what catches your eye. Investigate, explore, persist like a child. Ask questions. Make a note to look things up. Ponder why you're more curious about certain elements of your surroundings. Let your fascination guide you into untrodden territories - new forests, undiscovered trails, local hidden gems. And watch your world open up.

Activities to Try:

⊙ The Curiosity Adventure: Spend 1-2 hours on a wonder-walk you've never taken before. *This could be somewhere local you haven't been, a neighboring town, a new vacation spot, an unexplored area of the local state park.*
-Allow yourself to follow your curiosity rabbit.
-Journal, record or write a poem about where it lead you, and what you discovered.
-Journal anything unexpected that happened.

⊙ The Curiosity List: *Visit a library, bookstore or museum. Walk down the aisles, through the rooms.* Linger when a subject - book, object, painting, topic or idea - catches your eye.
-If you're in a bookstore, pick up the book or item.
-Record in your travel notebook everything that sparks curiosity, that made you stop and look.
-Select one or two items on your list to dive deeper into as a research or creative project.
-Journal if there is a pattern to the items on your list. What do they have in common? Why?

⊙ Imagination Triggers: During your Curiosity Adventure above, examine the subjects that triggered your interest - *that mysterious man in a hat, a strange door in a hedge, a cryptic sign.* Imagine what they might be about, their stories, journeys, secrets. Journal this: make it funny, poignant, let your imagination run wild. (Read <u>The Triggering Town</u> [*see* Bibliography] for observation and writing exercise ideas.)

Buzzing with ideas or enjoyed a 'Follow The Rabbit' activity recently? Record them below:

Journal This:

What were you curious about on your wonder-walk today? Why do you think it's fascinating to you right now?

What did you discover when you followed your curiosity rabbit? Describe the highlights.

DId anything unexpected happen? What would you do differently next time? What would you repeat?

Explorer's Notes

Related Cards:

How can you pair these related cards for a more interesting 'Follow The Rabbit' Wonder-Walk?

Portals, Hidden, Edges, Disruption

Explorer's Notes

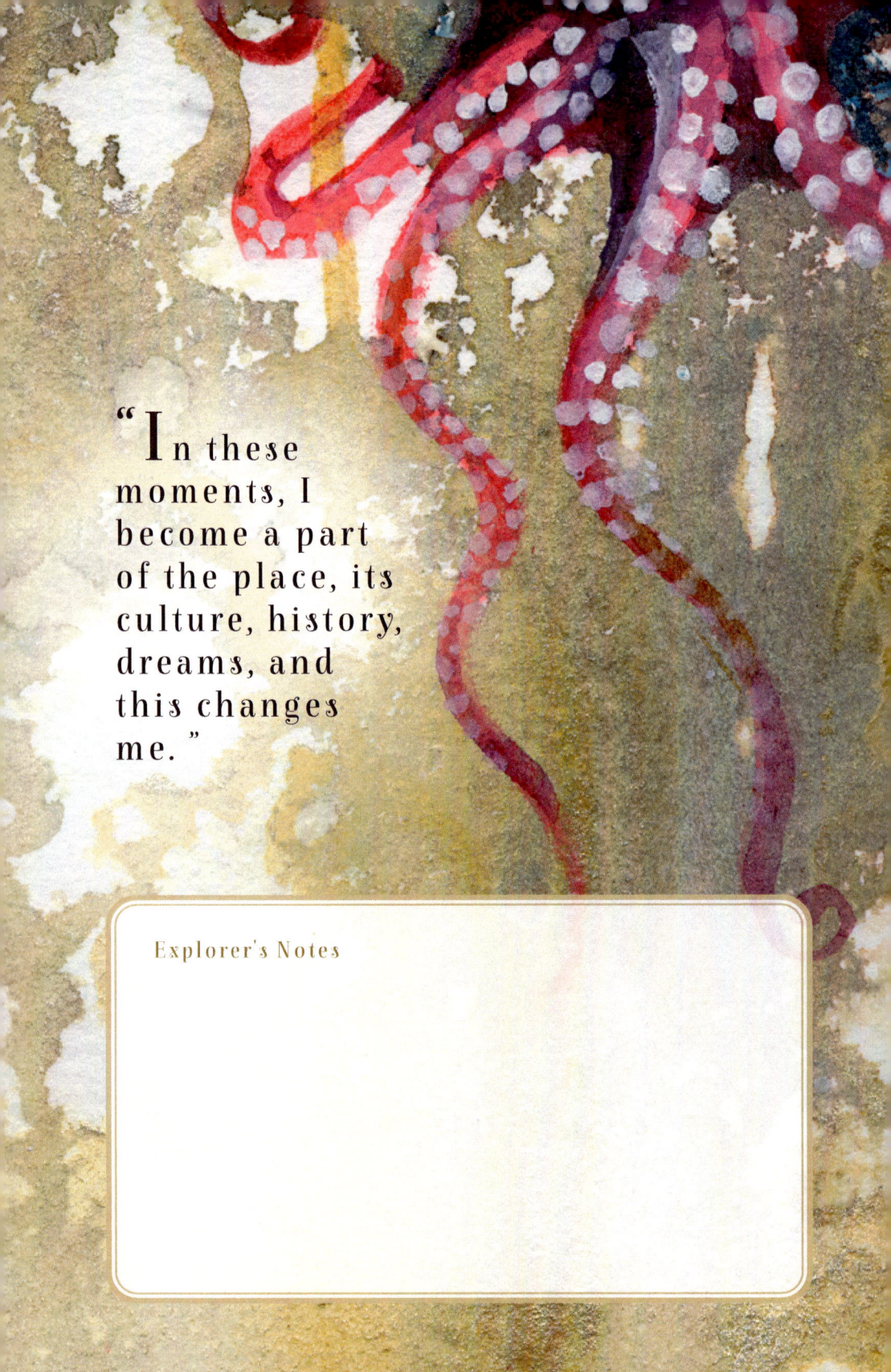

"In these moments, I become a part of the place, its culture, history, dreams, and this changes me."

Explorer's Notes

Immersion

Soak it all in, touch, taste, feel, learn.
What worlds do you want to immerse yourself in on your walk?

I treasure the times when I am immersed in a wonder-walk so captivating that it feels like I've been transported to another time and place. I am removed completely from my day-to-day milieu and dropped right into a bubble of sensory, creative and intellectual delights. A glass conservatory of rare, exotic tropical plants. A visit to a medieval town in France. A tour of ancient temple ruins overgrown with strangling fig trees. In these moments, I become a part of the place, its culture, history, and dreams, and this changes me. What immersive experiences can you seek out? Will you too be different after?

Interpretations:
Captivation, enthrallment, enchantment
Transported to another time or place
Deeply engaged, absorbed or involved
Concentration to the exclusion of everything else

Realm Symbolism:
Secret Garden: The Influence Realm
Corresponding Symbolism: Air, Intellect, Thinking
Ask: How does 'Immersion' enhance your walk?

Observe This on Your Wonder-Walk:

Observe your entry into immersion. What is the threshold between inside and outside? Notice the moment you become so completely enthralled that you felt like you were entering another world. Did it happen gradually or immediately?

What physical traits, atmosphere or characteristics make this such an immersive experience? Is it the architecture? The geography of place? Was it the way it was designed, like Walt Disney's vision for his parks? As you wander around, what are you noticing, thinking and feeling?

Observe your exit from this immersion. Notice how you feel about leaving it behind. Would you miss it? What do you wish you were bringing with you back into the everyday world?

Activities to Try:

⊙ A Faraway Land: Plan an adventure to an immersive environment near you where you can spend at least 1-2 hours - *a themed amusement park, a quaint historic town, a botanical garden, a conservatory, an aquarium, etc.*
-Wonder-walk the place.
-Journal how the atmosphere, mood and physical environment changes as you enter or exit this place. Record how you feel throughout.
-Write a story or poem about your experience. Take photographs or sketch what captivated you the most.

⊙ Obsessive Immersion: Look through your journal entries from the activities in this book, or from your wonder-walks notes for ideas.
-Select a subject that you've repeatedly found fascinating. Perhaps it's forests, fairy tales or the cultural history of your area.
-Immerse yourself in this subject for at least a week. Visit a library or a museum to find out more about it. Read and watch related movies or documentaries. Find ways to be involved in the physical environments of your subject matter. Give yourself permission to obsess over it.
-Journal your feelings, ideas and discoveries.

Buzzing with ideas or enjoyed an 'Immersion' activity recently? Record them below:

Journal This:

When was the last time you felt completely and enchantingly immersed in a place or experience? Describe it as vividly as possible. How did you feel? What was captivating? How did it change you once you left the place?

What are some of your favorite immersive places near you? Why and how do they transport you?

If you could pick one place to immerse in, where would it be? What do you crave about it?

Explorer's Notes

Related Cards:

How can you pair these related cards for a more interesting 'Immersion' Wonder-Walk?

Belonging, Roots, Edges, Dream

Explorer's Notes

"If we could get lost anywhere in the world, wouldn't it be better to get lost where it matters most?"

Explorer's Notes

Discernment

Discernment is a sharpening of perception.
Can you filter out the noise and focus only on what matters?

As an enthusiastic explorer, I've long since realized there will
not be enough lifetimes for all the wondrous adventures I
could embark upon. Discernment is the creative soul's secret
weapon to conserving energy, by letting into our treasure
box of a life, only the experiences that are most joyful and
meaningful. If we could get lost anywhere in the world,
wouldn't it be better to get lost where it matters most? This
card invites us to be discerning about our everyday walks, to
ask: what experiences serve our journey best? What would
make us feel most alive?

Interpretations:
Good judgment of information
A sharpened point of view, voice, perception
Clear-sightedness, focus
Critical, particular; sensitive

Realm Symbolism:
Secret Garden: The Influence Realm
Corresponding Symbolism: Air, Intellect, Thinking
Ask: How can 'Discernment' enhance your walk?

Observe This on Your Wonder-Walk:

What places do you look forward to immensely, counting
down the hours until you can run out the door for your walk?
Perhaps it's your secret beach hideaway at dusk, the botanical
gardens you get lost in for hours, the musty used bookstore in
town. Notice the places you can't wait to escape to, how they
replenish your thirsty soul every time you experience them.

As you walk, notice what in your environment gives you most
joy. Observe how certain elements heal and nourish you. Is
it the trees and its calming presence? The quiet serenity of a
tidal pond? Inspiration in floor to ceiling books?

Do these sanctuaries change from season to season? Does your
enjoyment depend on how you're feeling or who you're with?

Activities to Try:

⊙ Sanctuary Cards: Create a deck of cards featuring your most nourishing wonder-walks and places. Reach for it to inspire adventures that boost and heal your spirit.
-Cut out a set of cards about 3" x 5" in size, or use blank index cards.
-On one side of the cards, paste a picture you've taken of the sanctuary. You can also collage, paint or sketch it. Write the name of this place below the picture. You can also name it something whimsical and personal to you.
-On the reverse side of the cards, write a short blurb about why this place is special to you.
-Make a card for each sanctuary or wonder-walk locations in your area.

⊙ Sanctuary Walk: Use the cards you just made together with your Wonder-Walking Card deck. Select the location/sanctuary that aligns most with what you're needing in your journey right now. *A quiet place to sketch ideas for a new collection? A place to study birds for the book you're writing? A scenic walk to take your mind off some troubles?* It's okay to mix things up every now and then with new places, but know that you can dip into this nurturing deck anytime you need to come alive.

Buzzing with ideas or enjoyed a 'Discernment' activity recently? Record them below:

Journal This:

What is most important to you in the next 6 months to a year?
Is it your family? A creative project? Community engagement?

What wonder-walks, adventures or experiences would serve
this particular moment of your journey best? Why?

If you could cut out 3 distracting activities to make room
for more meaningful experiences, what would they be? What
would you replace them with?

Explorer's Notes

Related Cards:

How can you pair these related cards for a more interesting
'Discernment' Wonder-Walk?

Height, Story, Intuition, Journey

Explorer's Notes

"She is a *tabula rasa*, a chance for do-overs, all bright-eyed and bushy-tailed possibility."

Explorer's Notes

Dawn

Dawn is not just the rising of the sun, but a beginning, an emergence, a new day. What comes alive at this time?

Dewdrops glistening on leaves, a lazy early morning mist, the hushed hum of a world slowly waking up - dawn steals my breath every daybreak. To me, she is a *tabula rasa*, a chance for do-overs, all bright-eyed and bushy-tailed possibility. Dawn is a gentle crossing from the ethereal dream world of sleep into the dazzling liveliness of reality; an easing of darkness into light, within and without. What comes alive at dawn? How do we honor her? Begin as you mean to go on, this card seems to whisper. Set the tone for the rest of the day, and all will be well.

Interpretations:
Morning, daybreak
A fresh beginning
Tabula rasa - clean slate
Possibility, hope
Epiphany, clarity, realization

Realm Symbolism:
Secret Garden: The Influence Realm
Corresponding Symbolism: Air, Intellect, Thinking
Ask: How would 'Dawn' enhance your walk?

Observe This on Your Wonder-Walk:

How does walking in the early hours of dawn different from other times of the day? How is the blue twilight hour just before the sun rises distinct from the similar one just after sunset?

Observe what around is you waking up. Do you hear the chirping morning birdsong, a rooster crowing, shopkeepers getting ready for the day? Notice what interesting happenings you'd be missing if you were still in bed.

Observe the quality of light, is the sky a rosy pink tinged from the rising sun? Is it quieter? More serene? Bustling with the city starting its day? Notice if experiencing dawn changes the way you choose to walk into the day before you.

Activities to Try:

⊙ Overnight Camping Trip: Plan a weekend away to a secluded camping spot you haven't been to. Walk-in, 'primitive' camping spots are best, as they are more isolated from RVs and other campers.
-Arrive at your camping spot after dark. Set your alarm to wake up just before the sun rises.
-The next morning, savor and soak in the serenity of dawn with only nature for company as you make your morning coffee over the campfire.
-Notice how daylight changes this strange new place you only saw in the dark the night before.
-Notice the quality of morning light around you, from the time it peeks through the horizon and spills into the sky in dazzling colors.
-What other creatures are waking up along with you?

⊙ An Early Morning Picnic: Set out for your daily stroll a few hours earlier than you normally would, in the wee hours of the morning just before the sun rises. Select a spot, perhaps on higher ground, that allows you a good view of the sun rising over the horizon.
-Bring along a flashlight to navigate in the dark.
-Pack a thermos of coffee or tea, a warm cozy wrap and a blanket to sit on.
-Bring along a camera, travel notebook, journal or your painting kit.
-Observe how it feels to witness this familiar environment at dawn. Record what changes around you, the sounds, sights, smells, mood as the sun rises. Do you feel more excited for the day?

Buzzing with ideas or enjoyed a 'Dawn' activity recently? Record them below:

Journal This:

Describe a recent time you experienced the magic of dawn in a big way. Where were you, and why were you outdoors this early?

What is your favorite activity to do first thing in the morning, at the break of dawn? Why and how does it set the tone for the rest of the day?

If you could take a wonder-walk every morning to watch the sun rise, where would it be? Why this place?

Explorer's Notes

Related Cards:

How can you pair these related cards for a more interesting 'Dawn' Wonder-Walk?

The Sun, Naiveté, Darkness, Dusk

Explorer's Notes

"**W**hat do we know about the invisible worlds right under our noses?"

Explorer's Notes

Hidden

There is a rich world in the hidden. What is unseen hides kingdoms. What are you drawn to unconvering?

I wonder about the tangle of tree roots beneath the ground. I am simultaneously terrified of the horrific creatures of the ocean abyss and the visceral clarity of my harbored dreams. What is hidden is at once terrible, wondrous, mysterious, and intoxicatingly fascinating. Our imaginations are heightened by the unseen, our minds conjure stories from the merest of ghostly hints. What do we know about the invisible worlds right under our noses? What secrets can we discover for ourselves in an overexposed world? This card invites us to seek our own answers, to see and judge with our own eyes what rightly shines in light, and what's best kept hidden in the dark.

Interpretations:
Invisible, unseen, buried
Secrets, concealed, private
Obscure, mysterious, more than meets the eye
Not yet known, to be discovered

Realm Symbolism:
Secret Garden: The Influence Realm
Corresponding Symbolism: Air, Intellect, Thinking
Ask: What 'Hidden' wonders would enhance your walk?

Observe This on Your Wonder-Walk:

As you walk, look out for interesting happenings hiding in plain sight. What wonders are concealed behind that ominously closed gateway? What lives beneath the murky waters of the ocean? What are trees whispering to each other in the complex network of fungi and roots under your feet?

Are there hidden gems in your town or city you've never visited? How can you seek them out? As you saunter, ponder the secrets your own heart hides from you, leaving clues in the form of curiosity and fear. Look all around you for physical signs that there is more than meets the eye - a blink-and-miss sign to an underground cave, an unmarked road to the beach, a pop-up breakfast spot. Is it more exciting for being obscured?

Activities to Try:

⊙ Hidden Gems: Make a list of hidden gems in the area you live right now, the magical places and experiences only locals know about. Some ideas:
Favorite local trails/hikes
Speakeasies
Niche, underground museums
Secret Gardens or forests
Unmapped vistas and scenic lookouts
Food pop-ups or supper clubs
-Which ones have you visited? Which would you like to explore or reconnect to? Make plans to go.
-Before you enter this place, imagine, speculate, guess what it might be like based on physical clues.
-Journal if it meets expectations, is it better or worse for being hush-hush? Did you guess right?

⊙ A Hidden Sanctuary: Remember the treehouses, secret clubs and hideaways we created as children? Where we kept our most treasured books, games and toys? There is something wonderful about having a private sanctuary to escape to as needed. Where can you built or set this magical space up?
Consider beautiful grown-up canopies and tents in a corner of your house. A folding screen. A backyard shed. A private balcony. A fairy house made from nature's gifts in your favorite tree.
Assign this place and have fun making it your own!

Buzzing with ideas or enjoyed a 'Hidden' activity recently? Record them below:

Journal This:

Describe your favorite hidden gem in the place you live right now. Why do you think it's remained a local secret? What is special about it?

What hidden worlds both fascinate and scare you at the same time? Why? Describe what you imagine it to be.

What hidden places and interests would you most like to explore right now? Why?

Explorer's Notes

Related Cards:

How can you pair these related cards for a more interesting 'Hidden' Wonder-Walk?

Darkness, Portals, Roots, Fog

Explorer's Notes

"Look out for signs that the land holds memories of those that lived there before you."

Explorer's Notes

Memory

What memories are embedded in the world around you?
What are you being reminded of?

In the age of orality, before we were literate societies, memory
kept humans alive. We took great pains to remember not only
places, plants and animals that nurtured us, but also ones to
avoid. We memorized vast stretches of landscape so we could
find food, water and shelter when needed. It may be difficult
to imagine today what it was like when memory and land
intertwined in a beautiful song of survival. Thankfully, like
our ancestors, our stories remain entangled with the lands
we've walked and made home, though it must be consciously
sought. This card invites us to recall these embedded
memories - ours, and the ones that belong to those before us.

Interpretations:
Recollection, remembrance, reliving
Mental retaining of events, facts or impressions
To keep alive, preserve or make last
Consciousness of a time past

Realm Symbolism:
Secret Garden: The Influence Realm
Corresponding Symbolism: Air, Intellect, Thinking
Ask: How would 'Memory' enhance your walk?

Observe This on Your Wonder-Walk:

As you walk, notice if your impression of a place or experience
is colored by a memory or association with something in the
past. If so, why are you being reminded of it?

Walk your surroundings as if you're trying to memorize it for
later - imagine you're moving away, or trying to describe it to
someone who has moved away. Notice what you'll miss most if
you had to leave it all behind. Why?

Look out for signs that the land holds memories of those that
lived there before you. A stone hearth, an abandoned cottage,
a broken-down carriage in the wild. What do you think
happened? Can you imagine what life was like back then?

Activities to Try:

- The Memory Walk: Inspired by Hannah Hinchman, and similar to the 'Landmarks' card activity on memory-walking, select a meaningful place from a recent memory, or as far back as childhood. *Your grandparents' house, a hometown library, your high school.* Imagine yourself back in this place, recall the feelings, environment, sights, smells, sounds. On a blank page, map out what you see and feel as you memory-walk your way through the place. Review your notes after - what long-forgotten tidbit did you remember from 'memory-walking' this place? What's now altered?

- The Encoding Walk: In the book The <u>Memory Code</u> (*see* Bibliography), Lynne Kelly discusses an incredible memorization technique used throughout history, sometimes called "Method of Loci", where information is encoded into the land and recalled at will.
  -Select your favorite daily wonder-walk route and an unrelated list of information you've been wanting to memorize - *e.g. 100 local birds of your county.*
  -A sequence of physical locations (*a rose bush, the orange mailbox, etc.*) along your walk is defined, and each item on your memory list is 'embedded' (associated) with it.
  -Recite these associations every time you walk by. Create songs, stories or entire mythologies to help you remember the information encoded.
  -Observe any interesting connections or patterns that arise from your Encoding Walks.

Buzzing with ideas or enjoyed a 'Memory' activity recently? Record them below:

Journal This:

What is your fondest memory of a place? Go back to childhood if necessary. Why? Make a list if you have more than one.

What do you miss most about these places?
Do you feel a sense of 'hiraeth' for it? (i.e. missing a time or place that no longer exists)

If you were to move away next week, what fond memories would you have about where you live right now?

Explorer's Notes

Related Cards:

How can you pair these related cards for a more interesting 'Memory' Wonder-Walk?

Landmark, Spirit of Place, Home, Dream

Explorer's Notes

Explorer Notes from Part II:

What have I learned from Part II?

PART III

Wonder Rhythms & Rituals

The Wonder-Walk
(Single Card Pull)

Start here. This is the best way to get to know your brand new walking cards, as it is simple and easy to remember. Pull a single card randomly from a deck of freshly shuffled cards, face down.

Turn it face up to see your wonder-walk for the day: study the card's colors, textures and mood. *How does it make you feel? What does it remind you of?* Note the prompt on the card and what Realm it belongs to. From here on, you can let the prompt guide you intuitively on what to observe and contemplate during your walk, or you can look the card up in this book for more guided interpretations, activities and explorations.

Variations:
- Pull the card you're drawn to from a pile, face up.
- Pull a card Reflection-style - *after* a walk instead of before, as a way to interpret and remember it.

Wonder-Walk Adventure Spreads

You see, these quiet moments create an enveloping, immersive, creative solitude in which I can finally hear my own voice.

It's certainly not necessary to have a special deck of cards to enjoy wonder-walking. However, I can't deny that these cards inspire me to consider my strolls in ways I haven't before, especially when familiarity has set in and I stop being fully present - like all the times I've walked away from my car wondering two minutes later if I'd locked the doors, or when I drive away for a holiday worrying if I'd turned the gas stove off.

I appreciate how the cards make my daily walks fresh and interesting each time, but also how I can use them to recall my feelings after a particularly moving adventure. Most importantly, they help me stay mindful on my jaunts, sparking meaningful contemplation along the way.

In this chapter I share with you my favorite ways to use the cards, from a simple getting-to-know you practice, to more complex adventure-planning and musings of your next holiday trip. These adventure spreads are fun whether you read the cards intuitively (without looking up meanings), or use the Part II section of this guidebook to spark deeper explorations.

On Seeing Pictures: Word vs. Image

One of the comments I get most about the cards is how small the word prompt is. After trying it out in various sizes, I realized I preferred it small because I'm often distracted by large type on oracle and tarot cards I collect. As a visual intuitive, I love when the beautiful imagery of a card is the first thing I notice, as this aids my interpretation when I ponder the prompt.

Explore reading your cards this way in all of the spreads here if you're usually drawn to words. Compare which way frees you up to 'see' the magical adventures your soul needs most right now.

A Pair To Dance
(Double Card Spread)

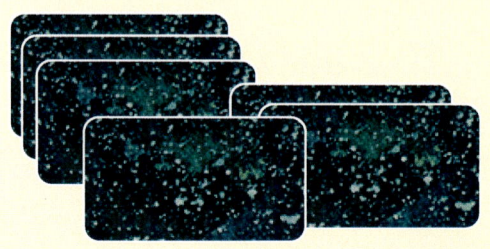

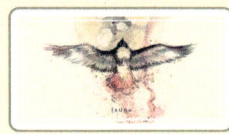 

This is a fun adventure spread to try out with a fellow wonder-walker, though it's just as fun by yourself. Pull two cards (one each for you and your companion) from a freshly shuffled pile, face down.

Turn the cards face up and study their color, texture, mood and prompt like you would a single card. Note what Realms they belong to. Intuitively compare the two cards: *How are they similar or different? Do they juxtapose or complement each other in interesting ways? E.g. If you pulled "Fauna"(The Creative Realm) and "The Woods" (The Inner Realm), a wonder-walk might involve observing and sketching your spirit animals in a nearby woodland.* Get creative: see if you can connect your two cards for whimsical, funny or surprising walks!

Variations:
- Pull the cards you're drawn to from a pile, face up.
- Divide the card deck into Realms and draw each card from a different Realm for more contrast.

The Labyrinth Adventure
(Four Card Spread)

I love this spread for longer wonder-walks or weekend creative adventures, especially when I find myself in a new city or area. Pull four cards from a freshly shuffled pile, face down.

Turn the cards face up and study each card's color, texture, mood and prompt, individually and together as a group. *Is there an overarching pattern or message? Which card stands out most? How do they interact with each other?* Design an adventure using these four cards as a guide, letting the Realms gently 'flavor' the adventure: *e.g. "Flora", "Dusk", "Follow the Rabbit" and "The Woods" could be an adventure in a nearby woodland ("The Woods" as the standout card) at sunset, where the color or plant life is most creatively inspiring. Let your 'curiosity rabbit' guide you to the exact spot to wander.*

Variation:
- Divide the card deck into Realms and draw each card from a different Realm for more contrast.

The Adventure Reflection
(Open Card Spread)

This is the spread to reach for if you don't feel like pulling a card before a wonder-walk or an adventure. Instead, draw these cards on location right after, or when you've returned home, settled and cozy. Hold the deck in one hand, face up, and flip through card by card, selecting ones that immediately represent your feelings about your trip, until you have a pile of no more than 12 cards (less is totally fine).

Begin culling this pile down to a smaller pile of 3-6 cards. Eliminate cards that don't resonate strongly with the experience by asking: *What was this trip about? How did I feel when I was there? What does it remind me of? What did I enjoy most about it? How was it memorable? What stood out most on this trip?*

Journal the final cards intuitively, or with the help of this guidebook to discover if your adventure was meaningful or enlightening in any way.

Explorer Notes for Adventure Spreads:

Do you have a special wonder-walk or adventure
spread that you've created or modified? What are
some of your favorite variations and tweaks?
Sketch or note them here for future reference.

"I am as much a part of nature's cycles as the plants and wildlife around me. I am subject to the same seasonal cadences."

Walking Through the Seasons

Some days I'm skipping all the way, and some days I drag my feet. But I go. And it is always rewarding.

The kinds of wonder-walks we take naturally shift with the year's seasons. As the weather changes from cold to warm, from dry to humid, from bleak, barren, brown to explosions of vivid color, so do we, like all our fellow creatures that belong to the land. We can't help that our mood swings depending on the amount of sunshine, fog or rain we're exposed to.

Even if we've become much less dependent on our environments for survival - an unceasing drought no longer means certain famine in fall, and shelters do not easily wash away in heavy rain - we still feel the seasons in our bones.

For many years I found myself frustrated at the end of the year when summer crept into fall; as the days shortened and cooled, so did my my energy. I wanted to curl up and read, daydream instead of furiously paint like I did all summer. I no longer felt like running outdoors with my camera, preferring to slip into long, leisurely walks with no expectations of photography, sketching or journaling. I didn't understand that my body was responding to an ancient rhythm, and felt betrayed by its refusal to keep going.

Eventually I realized I am as much a part of nature's cycles as the plants and wildlife around me. I am subject to the same seasonal cadences.

This chapter is about finding your own wonder-walking rhythms and remembering what it's like to be a part of the cycle of life on Earth. We'll do this by creating Explorer Charts that honor our bodies' attunement to the shifting seasons, so that our adventures nourish us in the ways we need most.

Seasons	Intentions	Amy's Explorer Notes
WINTER January, February, March	Recentering Visioning Planning	*I'm re-establishing who I am and what's important to me as I begin to visualize and plan what I want in the journey ahead.* During this time, I like revisiting my dreams, values, personal myths, and point of view. The natural world around me is asleep, a serene backdrop for walks and adventures that help me recenter myself and reaffirm what's important to me and my intentions for the year.
SPRING April, May, June	Wonder Aliveness Exuberance	*I've begun diving into the big projects of the year; excited beginnings are vibrating all around me.* The warmer weather, rain and blooming wildflowers coincide with my soul-need to refill my creative well. I seek out new walks and adventures that spark fresh inspiration for art projects ahead.
SUMMER July, August, September	Creativity Adventure Challenge	*By summer, I've settled into an easy rhythm. This season is about pushing myself out of my comfort zone and taking on new challenges.* I'm usually most creatively productive in summer, choosing projects that stretch me beyond my usual limits. Energy is high and the days are long, and so I seek out walks and adventures that nurture this boundlessness.
FALL October, November, December	Cocooning Reflection Rest	*I slow down in fall; the need to cocoon and renew is strong. This is my season of rest and deep replenishment.* Darkness arrives early, the days shorter and cooler, and the abundant energy of summer is waning. I feel an unmistakable need to withdraw and review the year so far. I seek out contemplative walks and adventures that nourish my soul and help me reflect.

The Labyrinth of Enchantment

Moonlight walk + picnic

Sketch trees in the wild

Sunset beach stroll

Mood-paint forests

Dawn hike

Photograph wildflowers

Spring Magic

Study local salt marsh

Walk in the quiet night to hear inner thoughts

Identify native plants by name

Try walking meditation

Visit Monet in museums

Journal after walks

An Explorer's Chart

Explorer Notes:

Big ideas for walks and adventures? Note them here.

Creating Your Own Explorer Charts

Your seasonal Explorer Charts will probably look nothing like mine. Our bodies respond differently to the changes in the seasons, depending on where we call home, or where we are in our current life journeys.

Perhaps you live in a part of the world where wonder-walking is unrealistic for many months, like long, dreary winters, or sticky, sweltering summers. For example, I grew up in the tropics just north of the Equator where it was unpleasantly hot and humid all year. Walks were usually dawn and dusk affairs, when temperatures were cooler and more agreeable.

By creating and using our Explorer Charts, we learn to work with our own rhythms and shifting local conditions so that adventuring is enjoyable no matter the season.

Charting Explorer Rhythms & Intentions

Using my example on the previous pages, chart how you naturally move through the year as your tasks, climate and environments shift.

Download and print a blank Explorer's Chart from your *Secret Explorer's Library* (see Resources at the end of this guidebook) and create one for each season.

You can include favorite activities, wonder-walks and Adventure Spreads from this guidebook, or just jot down in the appropriate Realms what you're looking forward to experiencing around you during these few months, especially if they're seasonal, like wildflower hikes, annual festivals or wildlife sightings.

Pin your chart where you can see it every day so you can be inspired to wonder-walk all year round!

Journal This:

What are you often drawn to doing during this season?

What wonder-walks, adventures and activities will support and nourish you this cycle?

Have fun. Map this out in your Explorer's Chart.

Explorer Notes for Seasonal Walking
How does your adventuring change with the seasons?
Chart your own rhythms and cycles here.

"We form stronger, more sustainable communities because our adventures show us how we're all connected in this tapestry of life."

Enchanted Exploring Your Way

*Nothing is more powerfully centering than
the meditative rhythm of walking.*

I can hardly believe we've arrived at the final chapter of this guidebook to wonder-walking. I hope by now you feel less intimidated by the idea of venturing into the wild, maybe even excited by where you'll go and what you'll see on your next evening stroll. If you've come away from this guidebook with nothing but a simple determination to overcome inertia and walk 5 minutes a day, my work is done, and this has all been worth it.

Before we part ways, I want to leave you with a few thoughts to ponder as you deepen your enchanted exploring. In the following pages, I share additional tips to help you understand more intimately your own path to wonder, as well as how you can help others in your community do the same.

At the beginning of this guidebook I had one simple wish: to show you a few ways wonder-walking restores enchantment and creativity into my everyday. Now that we've been through so much together, I want to share why I believe this simple ritual is so important to the future of humanity.

I believe that the more we wonder-walk, the more sensitive we become to ourselves and the land around us. We are alert to what feels right or wrong because our walks provide the stillness needed to listen to our intuition. We relax into the land as we walk, which allows our creativity to flow. We form stronger, more sustainable communities because our adventures show us how we're all connected in this tapestry of life, that everything we do matters and has real consequences. A conscious humanity is a caring one. I look forward to that world.

Thank you for wonder-walking with me.

Understanding How You Explore

While the cards in *A Deck for Wonder-Walking* provide ample inspiration for delightful adventures, it's not always obvious why some walks are more satisfying than others. The journal prompts below provide an additional guide to understanding your own explorer rhythms so that you know when and what to modify for a more sustainable and nourishing practice.

Journal This:

How do you like your daily walks? Short, long, morning or evening? Planned or spontaneous?

How affected are you by changing local seasons (see previous chapter) and personal goals? When is it easier or harder to wonder-walk?

When or where do your most enjoyable walks happen? Are they accidental? Are they usually at a particular time of the day or in a particular place? Do they usually happen when you travel? Are you sharing this walk with someone else?

When or where do you find yourself immersed deeply in your environment? How long will you have to be there for this to happen? What other conditions in your environment encourage this?

When or where are ideas and epiphanies most likely to bubble up on your walks?

When or where are your walks most soothing and healing to the soul?

Creating a Wonder-Walking Circle

Wonder-walking in a circle of kindred spirits is a beautiful way to experience how similarly (or differently) we respond to our physical worlds. It's marvelous for fostering camaraderie because it provides interesting fodder for discussion and connection. *Consider how this would enhance your weekend hiking clubs, creative and business retreats, or even Sunday brunch meetups.*

A Physical Realm Group Activity Idea:
Draw a Physical Realm card for the whole group, e.g. "Height", and have everyone go on a wonder-walk. Upon return, take turns sharing how they experience "Height" through their senses. Discuss if or how everyone's perceptions differ in unique ways - a great ice-breaker!

A Creative Realm Group Activity Idea:
Draw a Creative Realm card from for the group, e.g."Textures". Have them select a creative medium - *photography, sketching, writing, etc.* that they'll use to express the 'Textures' on their wonder-walks. Regroup to discuss and compare creations. Great for artist circles!

An Inner Realm Group Activity Idea:
Draw a card from this suit for the group, e.g. "The Woods", and have them think of a problem that's been bothering them while they wonder-walk in a nearby wood, alert to symbolic encounters. Reconvene and discuss if, or how, the woods affect their contemplation - This walk fosters deeper connections between explorers.

An Influence Realm Group Activity Idea:
Draw a card for the group, e.g. "Journey", and have them go on a walk, keeping eyes and ears open for this concept in the wild - *a butterfly's metamorphosis, a historical pilgrimage in the area, etc.* Upon return, compare ideas for further research - great for writers and painters!

Explorer Notes from Part III:

What will I implement from Part III?

Bibliography & Resources

Books on Nature, Culture & Wandering

Ball, Philip. *Patterns in Nature: Why the Natural World Looks the Way It Does.* University of Chicago Press, 2016.

Ball, Philip. *The Self-Made Tapestry: Pattern Formation in Nature.* Oxford University Press, 2004

Choukas-Bradley, Melanie. *The Joy of Forest Bathing: Reconnect With Wild Places & Rejuvenate Your Life.* Rock Point, 2018

Emerson, Margaret. *Contemplative Hiking Along The Colorado Front Range.* Images and Adjectives Publishing, LLC, 2010

Gooley, Tristan. *The Lost Art of Reading Nature's Signs: Use Outdoor Clues to Find Your Way, Predict the Weather, Locate Water, Track Animals and Other Forgotten Skills (Natural Navigation).* The Experiment, 2015

Gooley, Tristan. *The Natural Navigator: The Rediscovered Art of Letting Nature Be Your Guide.* The Experiment, 2011

Kelly, Lynne. *The Memory Code: The Secrets of Stonehenge, Easter Island and Other Ancient Monuments.* Pegasus Books, 2018

Books on Journaling, Writing & Creativity

Addonizio, Kim. *The Poet's Companion: A Guide to the Pleasures of Writing Poetry.* W. W. Norton & Company, 1997

Hinchman, Hannah. *A Trail Through Leaves: The Journal as a Path to Place.* W. W. Norton & Company, 1997

Hinchman, Hannah. *A Life In Hand: Creating the Illuminated Journal.* Peregrine Smith, 1991

Hugo, Richard. *The Triggering Town: Lectures and Essays on Poetry and Writing.* W. W. Norton & Company, 2010

Mentioned Reads

Barklem, Jill. *The Four Seasons of Brambly Hedge*. Philomel Books, 1990

Blyton, Enid. *The Adventures of Pip*, Dean & Son, 1968

Blyton, Enid. *The Magic Faraway Tree Collection*. Dean & Son, 2013

Carroll, Lewis. *The Annotated Alice: 150th Anniversary Deluxe Edition (150th Deluxe Anniversary Edition)*. W. W. Norton & Company, 2015

Burnett, Frances Hodgson. *The Secret Garden*. HarperCollins, 2011

Flieger, Verlyn. *Tolkien on Fairy-Stories*. HarperCollins Publishers, 2014

Juster, Norton. *The Phantom Tollbooth*. Alfred A. Knopf, 2011

J. Smith, Sally. *Fairy Houses: How to Create Whimsical Homes for Fairy Folk*. Cool Springs Press, 2017

Tolkien, J.R.R. *The Lord of the Rings: One Volume*. Houghton Mifflin Harcourt, 2012

Further Resources

Secret Explorer's Library for charts and other printables: www.labyrinthofenchantment.com/explorers-journal-goodies/

Labyrinth Locator: www.labyrinthlocator.com

iNaturalist App: www.inaturalist.org

"I believe that the more we wonder-walk, the more sensitive we become to ourselves and the land around us."

Thank You,

My Kickstarter Backers and Fellow
Wonder-Walkers, for believing in me
before I did,
My Husband, for being my Always-and-
Forever Adventure Guide,
My Mom, for nurturing my childhood
spark of wonder and creativity,
My Dad, for being my biggest fan,
confidante and cheerleader,
My Assistant, Karin, for freeing up
precious time so I can make this happen,
My Editor, Stephanie, for helping me over
the finish line and massaging my writing
into the best version it can be.

Friends, Loved Ones and Kindred Spirits,
for all your enthusiasm and
encouragement.

I appreciate you.

All At Once, Original Oil on Canvas

www.adeckforwonderwalking.com

About the Author

Amy is an artist, nature lover, and wonder-seeker creating art and tools to enchant the everyday. She is deeply inspired by the natural world, mythology and labyrinths. Through her art and offerings she hopes to inspire folks to embark on wonder-filled adventures that sharpen their senses, fuel their aliveness, and renew their enchantment with life.

You can find Amy online sharing her magical paintings, wonder-walks, and creative adventures at www.amytwon.com and on Instagram: @amytwon.